AF228637

"Alyssa states, 'At its core, confidence is a decision…You decide or determine whether you are confident.' At MIT, we teach that being a confident entrepreneur is not something you are born with—it is a learned skill."

Trish Cotter
Executive Director & Entrepreneur in Residence
Director delta v accelerator & Senior Lecturer
Martin Trust Center for MIT Entrepreneurship

"Using neuroscience to analyze the fundamentals of confidence is an interesting and challenging task. Trying to grasp these concepts can be daunting for people, but by understanding the basics, one can dramatically improve their well-being and success. As a neurosurgeon and neuroscientist, I commend Alyssa for her ability to translate these complicated concepts in a way that enables people to gain control of their thoughts, and gain insights into their actions. This can have meaningful and lasting impacts on how people project themselves in their own mind, and in turn the mind of others."

Vivek P. Buch, M.D.
Computational Scientist, Translational Neuromodulatory, and
Complex Systems Laboratories
Chief Resident, Department of Neurosurgery
University of Pennsylvania

"A unique blend of real science and real life that empowers you to build confidence through small, sustainable actions. Wonderfully devoid of lofty, abstract concepts, it's a practical how-to guide for growth-minded humans, and it's essential for young workers and those charged with leading them."

Matt Robinson
Founder & CEO
Upfront

"In her teaching and writing, Alyssa has the ability to connect with and educate all types of people—even scientists, doctors, and staff at UPenn. Her insights work across fields, but in particular, I have seen entrepreneurs grow with confidence after embracing her practical tips and empowered mindset."

Michael D. Poisel, M.S., M.B.A.
Executive Director, PCI Ventures
University of Pennsylvania

"**Confidence is a Choice** combines relatable anecdotes, scientific insights, and actionable guidance for people who care about their impact on other people to consistently and conscientiously choose to act, react, and interact with confidence."

Julianne Zimmerman
Lecturer, **Tufts University**
Managing Director, **Reinventure Capital**

"Confidence is an undeniable key for successful diversity and inclusion, academic and professional accomplishment, and personal satisfaction and wellbeing. In a powerful and quick read, **Confidence is a Choice** scientifically explains how confidence works in the brain and impacts behaviors. It explains and empowers anyone wanting to create a greater sense of belonging for themselves and others."

Marinda E. Monfilston
Diversity Program Coordinator
Yale University

"Confidence is what fundamentally attracts, retains, and optimizes talent. Alyssa is the expert on how and why confidence works—not just because she knows the science behind it, but because she understands organizations and interpersonal dynamics. She is able to apply otherwise intimidating brain science to real, everyday situations that challenge confidence in the workplace and elsewhere. Alyssa helps individuals break through barriers by providing actionable ways to improve confidence for yourself, your team and anyone else you care about."

Tracy Burns
CEO
Northeast HR Association (NEHRA)

"It's hard to imagine being a truly effective parent, manager, mentor, coach, individual contributor, or leader in any capacity without reading this book. As a CEO and seasoned salesperson, I now feel empowered knowing specifically how to have the greatest impact—as well as raise the performance of my team and everyone else I care about."

Kathryn Rose
Founder/CEO
wiseHer.com

"As an authenticity expert, I can tell you that without genuine confidence no one can comfortably interact with others in person or online. Alyssa scientifically explains why and how to get the confidence needed to live your life to the fullest—and help coach others so they can, too!"

Ryan Foland
Speaker
Author of **"Ditch the Act"**

"A crisis of confidence is something most of us have experienced at some point in our life. With detailed research **Confidence is a Choice** shows us we aren't alone and that we can develop confidence as a skill. Alyssa's engaging writing style provides a proven roadmap to develop confidence awareness and skills. A must-read for anyone seeking to grow personally and professionally."

Mari Ryan, M.B.A., M.H.P.
CEO/Founder, **Advancing Wellness**
Award winning author, **"The Thriving Hive: How People Centric Workplaces Ignite Engagement and Fuel Results"**

"**Confidence is a Choice** shows what a big role confidence plays in everything we do and every decision we make. Alyssa Dver gives readers practical tools to build your confidence by diving deep into your values, how to take command of confidence-stealing situations, how to decide whether you are "confident enough," and why recognizing your weaknesses is a sign of confidence. This eye-opening book will give you the, well, confidence to handle anything that comes at you."

Michele Wucker
Bestselling author, **"THE GRAY RHINO: How to Recognize and Act on the Obvious Dangers We Ignore"**

"With easy-to-digest bites of science and sensible insight, Alyssa Dver provides a timely guide for any person who chooses to lead with confidence and to encourage confidence in others."

Pamela D. A. Reeve
Chair
The Commonwealth Institute

"If there is one thing that makes or breaks success, health, and happiness, it is confidence. So, if you want to create more confidence for yourself and other people, learn from the recognized expert, Alyssa Dver. Her unique blend of science, humor, and practicality will profoundly change the way you think, behave and feel."

Robin Farmanfarmaian
Professional Speaker and Entrepreneur
Author, **"The Patient as CEO"**
and **"The Thought Leader Formula"**

---

*"Combining empirical observations with cognitive science, Alyssa has written a vivid guide suitable for all ages and audiences—students, educators, managers, parents, coaches, professionals, job-seekers and many others—to understand those around them and be understood. With anecdotes and research, **Confidence is a Choice** empowers us to introspect, improve and empower others."*

Michelle Fan
Chair
Wharton Alumni Angel Network Boston

---

*"Alyssa masterfully brings together the research, practice, and tools in this all-encompassing confidence bible for everyone who is looking to thrive in life as the best version of themselves. The theory, explanations, and methods in **Confidence is a Choice** are easy to access, easy to connect with, and easy to implement into everyday life. This is the one-book-quiver for increasing leadership capacity in yourself and others."*

Evren Gunduz, Ed.M.
CEO & Co-Founder
Enjoy Life Education Inc.

*"Buy this book. Read this book. Then, prop it up in your workspace where you can see it every single day and repeat Alyssa's words, **Confidence is a Choice** as your mantra.*

I love the whole concept of confidence as a choice we make. We work with women who want to be speakers but too often they hesitate to put themselves out there. Make the choice to be confident."

Bobbie Carlton
Founder
Innovation Women

---

*"I've often wondered what gives people confidence. Are they born with it? Is it their upbringing? Life events? Finally, that question has been answered with Alyssa's newest masterpiece—**Confidence is a Choice**! Through data-backed science, Alyssa takes us through the thought process and behavioral indicators that enable people from all walks of life, to 'choose' confidence to empower their belief system and desired outcomes.*

I work with C-Suite executives from around the world. Confidence is a critical trait that sets the most successful apart. As Alyssa's research shows, it can truly make the difference between win or lose. In personal relationships, it can build a bridge of trust. Someone who is confident is like saying "I got this!" How wonderful to know we've all "got this" if we choose. I highly recommend this book for anyone who has ever dared to believe that anything is possible."

Maria Minniti
Senior Director
Wharton Executive Education

---

*"**Confidence is a Choice** teaches through both storytelling and scientific evidence. In my coaching practice, I work with entrepreneurs at all ages and stages, this book and Dver's work at American Confidence Institute provides me with practical tools that allow me to be a confidence role model and empower others to choose confidence for themselves."*

Jenn Crenshaw
Chief People Officer, **Prospero Health**
Executive Coach, **Regroup Coaching**

---

*"**Confidence is a Choice** is a must-read for anyone who would benefit from moving through the challenges of life with more confidence (read—everyone). As Alyssa states, 'A lack of confidence cripples productivity, innovation, focus, and trust.' This book is packed with the science and practical application tools to help you craft your confidence as a learned skill. You have more control than you think."*

Therese Padilla
President
Assoc. of International Product Marketing & Management

---

*"Alyssa has done it again and upped everything! From new insights, new research, new science, new ways of thinking, and new tools, I can say, with unabashed confidence, **Confidence is a Choice** presents the leading edge in both understanding and imparting this life-enhancing competence we ALL have the power to choose to tap."*

Lawler Kang
Founder, **League of Allies**
Author, **"Passion at Work"** and **"The E Ticket"**

---

*"**Confidence is a Choice** is a wow! In my world of non-profit philanthropy, confidence is indeed the key to creating a compelling mission, motivating volunteer leaders, and engaging donors. That there is brain science behind the decisions we make, how we present ourselves, and the success we have, magnifies the significant role confidence plays in both our personal and professional lives.*

Required reading for young people just starting their careers to senior executives who lead complex organizations, this fascinating book compellingly illustrates that confidence is always the best indicator of success. Bravo to Alyssa for writing such a compelling and relevant book."

Ann Louden
CEO
The Ann Louden Company
Author of the upcoming book: "**Connection as a Superpower: How Social Courage Gives You the Edge in Life and Love**"

"Confidence can be an elusive leadership topic...easy to see in others but sometimes harder to attain for ourselves. Alyssa brings cutting edge psychology, and social science all together in a simplified, enjoyable (even entertaining) way. Now anyone can learn to be a more confident leader, especially by helping others be more confident, too."

Kristin Viera Zecca
Director, Executive Programs & Lecturer
MIT Sloan School of Management

CONFIDENCE IS A CHOICE

Real Science.

Superhero Impact.

Alyssa Dver

Mind Full Press
a subsidiary of Z. Holden Bros. Publishing Group

Copyright © 2020 by Alyssa Dver

Published in the United States by Mind Full Press, a subsidiary of Z. Holden Bros. Publishing Group.

All rights reserved.

ISBN 978-0-9833927-2-9

All rights reserved. Except as permitted under the United States Copyright Act, no part of this publication may be reproduced or distributed in any form or by any means, or stored in a database or retrieval system, without the prior written permission of the copyright holders.

Company and product names mentioned herein are the trademarks or registered trademarks of their respective owners.

Confidence is a Choice books are available at special quantity discounts for corporations, not-for-profit organizations and academic use. Also available online or onsite: keynote presentations, workshops, eClasses, assessments, confidence coaching, and coaching certification.

www.AmericanConfidenceInstitute.com

info@AmericanConfidenceInstitute.com

Cover design by Ally Tuttelman
Production Management by Kristin Deegan

First edition
10 9 8 7 6 5 4 3 2 1

In the scientific pursuit to become our best selves,

the real proof is that we are here.

Table of Contents

Foreword **23**

Introduction...**29**

Part 1: CLARIFY **35**

The Confidence Crisis **37**

Knowledge Isn't Power Anymore—Making
Confident Decisions Is.................................... 37

Being Overinformed Causes
Underconfidence.................................... 38

Extrinsic Confidence Is Like a Carb 38

We Thought We Were Doing the Right
Thing 39

Our Brains Need Our Help 40

Fit Wits 41

The One Decision We Should Make, We
Don't 42

Defining Confidence.................................... **43**

The Look of Confidence 43

Consistent Confidence Characteristics...... 44

You Can Fake News but Not Confidence... 45

The Confidence Trinity: Authenticity,
Humility, and Trust.................................... 46

Introverts May Actually Be More Confident
.... 46

Close but Not Quite—The Confidence
Cousins 47

What Is NOT Confident.......................... 49

Confidence Imposters.......................... 50

Liar, Liar, Confidence on Fire.................... 52

Truth and Confidence 53

Self—or Better Yet—Personal Confidence 54

You Are Never 100% Certain.................... 55

Hacking Confidence.......................... 56

Part 2: CALIBRATE 59

Calculating Confidence 61
We're Addicted to Data 61
The Missing Measurement 63
The Confidence Quotient (CQ) 64
A Situational Assessment, Not a One and Done Test 65
Find Out Your CQ 66

Confidence Brain Science Made Simple 67
A Better Brain Without Pain 67
The Old But Not So Wise Brain Stem 68
Little Shop of Wants & Worries 70
Your Own CEO: The Prefrontal Cortex 72
Chief of Staff – The Amygdala 73
Bicycle Brain 74
The Big Three Confidence Fears: Failure, Regret, Rejection 79
It All Boils Down to Belonging 80

Confidence Villains & Kryptonite 83
Confidence Stealing Situations 83
Bonehead Behaviors 85
All Too Common Bullying 87
Criticism Can Crush Confidence 88
Confidence Itself Can Be Intimidating 89
Self-Induced Confidence Killers 89
Confidence Kryptonite 90
Sleep Washing 91

Metaconfident Thinking 93
Authentic Confidence Requires More Than Being Authentic 93
Thoughts About Thoughts 94
Thinking Is Harder Than You Think 95
Burpees for Your Brain 96
You Have Higher Power 97
Conditioning Confidence 97

Your Incredibly Powerful Brain Is Actually Plastic 99

Literally, You May Be Shocked 100

Making Confidence Your Default Choice 101

Part 3: CONTROL **103**

Master Your Mindset **105**

Mindset Impacts Everything 106

Ready, Mindset, Go 107

Talking to Yourself Isn't Crazy—Just the Opposite 107

Your Brain Will Thank You 108

Make Someone's Day Every Day 108

Blow Down a Negative Mindset with Three Little Things 109

Structures Are Mindset Spark Plugs 110

Stand Like Superwoman 111

Create a Confidence Collection 112

Small but Mighty Mindset Movements .. 112

*Accountabilibuddies** 113

Practice What We Preach 114

Identify Your Values & Value **115**

Words of Worth 115

Discovering Your Values 117

Write Your "Youlogy" 119

Self-360 120

Stretch Before and After You Do These Exercises 121

Needs & Wants **123**

We Want to Need 124

The Eight Key Confidence Indicators (KCIs) 124

Personal Confidence Dashboard & Plan . 125

Wants Are Desired, Not Required 128

Confidence Requires Constant Course Corrections 129

Needs/Wants Test................................ 130

Example Needs/Wants Test: Buying a New Car.. 130

Tame Triggers.................................... **133**

Please Don't Make Me Do That 133

Inside Out Pet Peeves 135

Who Are You Allergic To? 137

Not Just a Person, but Those Types........ 138

They're Human Just Like You 139

Override Autonomic Responses **141**

Mind Your Breath................................ 141

Balance Your Brain and Your Body Will Follow.. 142

Communication Is Confidence's BFF....... 143

Plan Not to Panic................................ 144

Shiny Notification Syndrome.................. 145

Thinking Time Outs.............................. 146

Brain Breaks 146

Talk Less. Sleep More. 147

Make Confident Decisions........................ **149**

Comparisons Can Create Confidence...... 150

Decide to Decide 150

Timing Is Everything, Including an Excuse 151

Decision Game Plan............................. 152

Listen to Your Gut............................... 155

Confidence Begets Confidence.............. 156

Stress Is a Signal................................ 157

Big Life Decision Checklist.................... 159

Example Big Life Decision Checklist: New Job 161

Everyone's Opinions Matter—Especially Yours 162

Part 4: COMMUNICATE **163**

Conveying Confidence **165**
Your Eyes Are Louder Than Your Mouth. 165
*What Does "Good Eye Contact" Really
Mean?* 166
Confidence Is in the Eyes of the Beholder 167
Your Face Is Talking Too 168
Mom Was Right—Shoulders Back 168
Bend It Like Beckham 169
Subservient Language & Upticks 169
Waste Words 170
*Exorcise Subservient Language and Waste
Words* 170
Breaking Bad with a Buddy 172
Corresponding Confidence 172
Net Neutral Means Not Personal 174
*Conscientious Confident Communication—A
Mouthful if You Can Say It Well!* 175

Part 5: COACH **177**

Helping Others Be Confident **179**
Do Unto Yourself First 179
Coaching as a Concept 181
Good Coach. Bad Coach. 181
Being Kind Isn't Necessarily Helpful 184
Don't Act Like a Doctor Unless You Are One
.... 185
Confidence Coaching Roadmap 185
ACI Confidence Coaching Playbook 186
Coaching Matters. 188

Confident Conclusions **191**

Bibliography **193**

Acknowledgements **205**

Small Group Book Discussion Guide **209**

American Confidence Institute Information 211

You can download all the tools within the book here:
www.AmericanConfidenceInstitute.com/Toolkit

Foreword

I only ventured into this undefined space because I was desperate. I am convinced it was the only way I could hear the universe calling through my own life's cacophony.

In 2008, my oldest son, Zak, was diagnosed with a serious neurological condition called dystonia. It took more than a year to diagnose and even the most accomplished neurologists were barely familiar with the condition. They had few answers about the cause or treatment. They would often say, "We just don't know," or "We *think* this will help." Meanwhile, they also told me they thought Zak would end up being paraplegic, with the *upside* that he might benefit from new, seemingly successful brain surgery.

Maternal courage propelled me to hunt down cross-discipline, mind-body information that is normally not shared across medical practitioners. Going outside of their own expertise is too risky for them, but not for someone uncredentialed such as I. I searched for the latest in neurological, psychological, and sociological research. I learned about Eastern medicine and physiological theories that are still popular after hundreds of years. I conducted my own social research and interviewed experts in various brain science fields, located across the world. When I vetted my conclusions back through the experts, they confirmed that I was right. They also confirmed that I knew more than they did in this area—and anyone else they were aware of. They started calling *me* for information.

In hindsight, I was perhaps naïve to think I could solve a medical mystery. I did not earn a Ph.D. nor am I any kind of trained scientist.

Beyond helping Zak, I was admittedly narcissistic. I had a subliminal desire to find personal purpose beyond what I could do within my marketing career. I yearned to matter more in the world than what a common executive title and so-so salary signified. I craved differentiation in the universe that would show I was contributing something of unique value.

Despite these selfish motivations, I was blessedly led to do something bigger than myself.

Besides enabling Zak to take control of his body, I found hard proof that everyone can control their confidence—and to a large extent—other people's, too.

My Grand Conclusion Is That Confidence Is Everyone's Superpower and Choice

In leading the American Confidence Institute (ACI), I have had the great privilege to share data, tips, and techniques that have so far empowered over 350,000 smart, hardworking people to take control of their confidence and to live more successfully, on their own terms.

Since my 2015 book, *"Kickass Confidence: Own Your Brain. Up Your Game.,"* new technologies have completely changed our understanding of the human brain. Five years is a neurological eon. Tests and treatments have been overhauled. Totally new medicines and devices have been created. While Moore's Law predicted that computing power would double every two years, Alyssa's Law (yet to be proven, but it does have a nice ring) predicts that we double our understanding of the human brain every annum.

In the past 5 years, *I've* also changed a lot—that is, applying this knowledge to myself as well as my clients by creating, testing, and tweaking ACI's tools and techniques. I've worked with people from all walks of life and professions. I've been graciously invited into the heads and hearts of so many purpose-driven, growth-minded people. Every one of these high performers are impressively successful from the outside, and yet they ALL commonly suffer from constant confidence erosion. It doesn't matter that they are accomplished CEOs, consultants, neurologists, or Air Force commanders. They may even have academic credentials from intellectual breeding grounds such as MIT, Wharton, or Harvard, or from brand name corporations, hot startups, and other high-performance organizations.

While the participants have impressed me with their brilliance, commitment, and accomplishments, they also inspired me to continue my confidence quest. I know concretely that even the best and brightest need more confidence and they, too, are held back by a low Confidence Quotient™ (CQ).

They Don't Trust Themselves and Subsequently, They Make it Hard for Others to Do So, Too

Their discomfort with *who they are* leaks into all their relationships and shows up with every action, reaction, and interaction. It shows in their communication, reflects in their decisions, and defines their personality. They aren't seen as leaders or role models. This *disability* is visible to everyone like a scarlet tattoo labeling them, no matter what they wear. As the adage implies: *The suit doesn't make a man.* In reality, confidence does.

The Absence of True Confidence Denies Them Opportunities

People who lack confidence are passed over for promotions. They don't push themselves to seek new experiences because they worry they may fail or be unqualified. They stay safe by choosing compliance over creativity. They play their roles well within the confines of prescribed scripts. They live like programmed robots, to "get up and make the donuts," and "don't rock the boat."

But They Feel Bored and Fear They Are Boring

They are self-imprisoned by their own accomplishments. They are proud of WHAT they are, but they aren't happy with WHO they are. They don't have time to figure out how to change, plus they would risk everything they have worked so hard to earn. Changing how they operate is truly terrifying, seemingly insane. It is hardwired in how they've been taught to think and behave.

But when the symptoms become too painful—frustration, exhaustion, depression—they quickly blame it on age, circumstance, or bad luck. Deep down, they know that the source of stress is a lack of their own confidence. They aren't the person they want to be and have only themselves to blame.

If you relate to this firsthand, it may seem that you're alone with this shame. You may feel like the one person not living fully, wasting your potential, and just taking up space in the universe. I swear, you are not alone, and this is completely common.

I've Been Awakened to Know That Everyone Has a Story of Struggle and Everyone Is Human

Our confidence-related fears may manifest as arrogance, awkwardness, depression, subservience, shyness, indifference, or other forms of defensive survival. Instead, we too often accept, and even encourage, primitive survival behavior that seeks to steal and bully confidence from other people—especially in business. We then wonder why employee engagement is so low and why no one can be authentic or reach their full potential.

A lack of confidence cripples productivity, innovation, focus, and trust. It diminishes leadership, influence, and impact. It negates sales efforts and teambuilding. Toxic people take down organizations all because they lack confidence in themselves. Trace problems in any personal, professional, or political relationship and you'll find a lack of confidence at the core.

Confidence Should Be a Required Class

Shockingly, we aren't typically taught how to handle the everyday villains and kryptonite that weaken everyone's confidence—and they are getting worse. I believe we are in a confidence crisis that is at the heart of why we have epidemic social and political strife—from overdoses to dictators. With all our technological connectiveness, we now have too much information and too many choices. We're so distracted, overwhelmed, and exhausted that we can't make thoughtful decisions, let alone confident ones.

The Human Species is Not Evolving Fast Enough

To survive modern day mental challenges, we need to be much more emotionally adept and resilient. We urgently need to change how we think to accelerate the evolution of our brains.

With the #MeToo movement, gender equality, work life balance, employee engagement, and other proactive talent optimization movements, I am encouraged by the awareness and the intention to fix our personal and interpersonal misalignments. Schools and organizations are just now starting to teach critical social-emotional skills needed to cope with new world thinking.

However, the root of the problem still lingers. Life is tough and perpetually pokes us to act and achieve according to extreme social expectations. We have created a hypercompetitive world that pushes us to know more, be faster, be stronger, and leap over tall buildings but with very little patience or time. Our brains are wired to believe, act, and react in ways that are optimized for self-preservation which are often at the expense of other people's confidence and subsequent success. The solution is not a one-shot awareness exercise such as "calculating personality codes," "visualizing something that is desired," or "counting away your worries."

Your brain is smarter than that. It knows when you or someone else is trying to superficially create or fake confidence. Faking can be a productive form of practice, but it is not a sustainable way to think and influence. By gaining experience in something as a result of concentrated practice, you may become confident in that area only after you collect enough wins and other confirming rewards. True self-confidence comes from a factual understanding of what confidence is and how it works. It requires clarity of your own values, needs, and wants that then provides personal behavioral bumpers which keep you comfortably living within your own confident skin. Only then can you create the desired neurological pathways that activate desired habits and convincing communication. With your well-managed mindset, you can become a confidence role model and coach for other people, too. There is no better way to get confidence than to give it to someone else.

Therefore, this book is not just an update to my last one, but rather a transfer of responsibility to you as the reader.

I hope you, too, will choose to be a real-life superhero:
a Confidence Crusader.

Thank you for choosing to read this and helping to bring more confidence to the world.

Alyssa

Introduction

Confidence is power—and, it's not just renewable, it fuels other people's confidence. It's more controllable than karma and giving away confidence actually strengthens the source.

Confidence enables us to productively act, react, and interact. It directs every decision and behavior. When confidence is challenged, individuals are usually unaware if they go into survival mode. They act like cavepeople: irrationally, aggressively, and selfishly. Win or lose. Fight or flight.

I fundamentally believe that confidence is the cure for world peace, many diseases, and our epidemic unhappiness.

That may sound crazy, but what's really nuts is that others have known this for thousands of years.

Mindfulness, meditation, yoga, and other Eastern techniques have long aimed to elevate our cognitive awareness so we can better control our bodies and thoughts. Using modern technology, we now have Western medical proof that we can control our behaviors by having a calm, in-control, and confident brain.

Confidence Is the Key to... Well... Everything

Confidence is the actual secret behind the Law of Attraction. It is the fuel that allows us to pursue accomplishments and make decisions, especially things that aren't easy. An internet search returns several articles that state people make on average 35,000 decisions per day. Whether that number is accurate or not, we unquestionably make at least several thousand decisions every day including what to eat, wear, say, type, and think.

When someone is confident, they have real influence. They can more easily get what they want, value, and need. Authentic confidence enables authenticity, trust, and respect. Confidence gives leaders, managers, mentors, parents, friends, relatives, and citizens real influence. As we all scramble to find our Simon Sinek[1]-directed purpose, giving confidence is possibly the only one that matters.

Unknowingly, Everyone Has the Superpower to Unlock Their Own and Other People's Potential

Fictional superheroes are known to be mentally strong and selfless. They have unique strengths that allow them to persevere, despite venerable challenges and traumatic experiences. Their confidence is equally essential to help them override their vulnerabilities.

In the real world, no one is born confident. It isn't inherited through DNA or something you are lucky to just get. In fact, I will demonstrate in this book that confidence isn't even built or earned. It is not a feeling or an emotion, no more than being pregnant is.

Confidence Is a Choice–Definitionally and Neurologically

It is unfathomable that we aren't taught this and then stumble for at least 60 years to finally reach our confident best.[2] In fact, we are misled that intellectual talent and material accomplishment will effectively bring success. We're told that confidence is a result of being educated and working hard. We are indoctrinated with the belief that with enough practice, persistence, and patience, all will be well, and we will be rewarded with the spoils of success.

The Rules Are Wrong

Perhaps you are like me and followed that dogma. You did well in school, rounded out your resumé with extracurricular and charitable activities, got into a respected college, and maybe even went to grad school to further follow the apparently necessary roadmap. Eventually, you arrived in the real-world workforce with the tasks to find, land, and keep a decent job. There, you found a hodgepodge of people—some smarter than you, some not so much. Once in, depending on your industry, it may not have mattered at all where you went to school or the degrees you sweated to get.

More likely, your career progressed more by knowing the right person/people or by having lucky timing.

In your head, you still believe that you are truly a star player, and you continue to train to make yourself smarter, faster, and stronger. You attend professional conferences, read books, and listen to podcasts. You take all kinds of classes and watch TED Talks. You eat well, exercise, and maybe even practice mindfulness and meditation.

Outside of work, you text and drink with friends, check in with relatives, recycle, bake, and craft. You volunteer in the community, donate to meaningful causes, and you try to be a helpful neighbor. Date night with the honey, catch up on pop culture and the current sports scene. Deal with the dog, the bills, the house, the lawn, the laundry, and make investment decisions. Follow politics, music trends, and fashion. If you have children, you strive to be a super-parent by hiring tutors, shuttling them to extracurricular activities, arranging playdates, and booking memory-making family vacations. And oh yeah, don't forget to get everyone a flu shot. Shame on you for not making time for yourself!

You Never Feel You Are Doing or Being Enough

You live by the mantra "work and play hard," while you try to enjoy meaningful relationships, unplanned fun, and unassisted relaxation. You'll have plenty of time to sleep when you're dead. Carpe Diem. YOLO. Live every day like it's your last. You're pushing and pulling, moving and making as hard as you can.

That's what you are supposed to do. So then why are you so frustrated, unfulfilled, and unhappy?

This isn't the life you imagined. It's hard, exhausting, unforgiving, and too often, unfair.

Maybe you're bored, tired of the routine. You feel less than accomplished, overworked, and underappreciated.

You followed the rules, played the game, and committed the time. *So why did this happen?*

Many say this a classic mid-life crisis, but I see it happening to people at every age. You make a good enough living, but you don't have a good enough life.

Back in your own story, I bet you were adept at some task or understood a subject easily, so people said you were good at it. This gave you *situational confidence*. You declared a major, landed a great job, got on the professional fast track. Your aptitude created competence, and you followed those breadcrumbs to a career. Next thing you knew, you were promoted to a role that wanted more of your soul than your brain. Or worse yet, you got fired for being too experienced, too expensive, or too smart.

Maybe because you were such a great individual contributor, you were also tapped to manage others. Unfortunately, being smart and hardworking may impress others, but it doesn't inspire them. It can even make subordinates impatient, intolerant, and intimidated. A high IQ is not required to be a great leader, manager, parent, spouse, relative, or friend. And it turns out Emotional Intelligence (EQ) isn't the solution either.

Confidence Isn't a Result—It's a Requirement

Most people assume confidence comes through time and experience. Most also think that confidence is gained by practicing a specific task or exercising an ability.

Malcolm Gladwell argued that mastery and implied confidence comes from 10,000 hours of practice.[3] However, perfection-driven repetitive physical movement, often associated with professional musicians and athletes, can do just the opposite. Their intensity to achieve confidence in their craft can lead to dystonia—weakening their brain-to-body neural pathways.[4] The result is that the performers lose control of the parts of their own bodies needed to perform their craft. Disabled and unable to pursue their passion, it is a tragic irony that in their inspiring pursuit of perfect mind-body control, they are rewarded with crippled confidence.

Thankfully, with breakthroughs in brain science, we know there is an absolute possibility to retrain neural pathways. This treatment philosophy is already being applied to stroke victims, and massive amounts of research is being done to apply these same concepts to help neurological dysfunction caused by Parkinson's, Multiple Sclerosis (MS), Tourette's, and Alzheimer's. I have absolute faith that this holistic, but no less data-driven medical approach, will dramatically improve our ability to deal with and maybe even potentially avoid many debilitating diagnoses, from cancer to autism.

Own Your Brain to Succeed at Every Game

Luckily, confidence conditioning isn't painful, nor does it require special equipment or even a lot of money. Anyone can do it, but like improving any physical skill, mental training must start with willfulness. Paradoxically, it takes some confidence to become confident.

Please strap on your brain science-based seat belt, as this book is designed to quickly explain not just the *what* and *how* to have more confidence, but also *why* it works.

1. You will **CLARIFY** what confidence is and what it is not—both definitionally and neurologically. You will be able to recognize typical confidence-stealing villains and kryptonite.

2. You will then learn how to **CALIBRATE** confidence using simple but powerful brain science-based tools. You will identify specifically what is driving and holding back your confidence.

3. Next, by being armed with techniques to **CONTROL** confidence, you can protect your own and other people's confidence, too. Whether making a tough decision or

recovering from a life set-back, this section will give you both proactive and reactive confidence-empowering strategies.

4.   Once your mindset, values, needs, and wants are aligned on the inside, we'll discuss how to **COMMUNICATE** confidence to the outside world using your voice, body, face, and writing. The goal isn't just to appear more confident, but to be confident completely and consistently.

5.   Lastly, you will learn to be an everyday **COACH** who enables other people to be more confident, even if they didn't ask for help explicitly. Your confidence will inspire others with the courage to be their whole, happier selves.

I dream of a world where everyone can be confident—with a goal to prove to you, here, that it's possible.

Part 1: CLARIFY

The Confidence Crisis

From manipulated financial markets and political polls to fashion trends and all things technological—we live in a society that craves controversy, change, and the thrill of disruption. These societal factors stress our confidence as we try to keep up with the Joneses, Kardashians, and the proclaimed best practices at home and at work.

Knowledge Isn't Power Anymore—Making Confident Decisions Is

Five channels, no DVR, no cable, no streaming, no on-demand. Five salad dressings and only two options to sweeten your coffee—real or fake. If you remember those days, you know they were much easier. If you don't, go ask a boomer.

Today, our options are endless—the list is as long as the Amazon (River) and as worldwide as the web. We have so many choices, it's truly overwhelming. Psychologists call this *overchoice* or *choice overload*,[5] which means it can be difficult, if not impossible, to make a confident decision when presented with too many options.

It's not that we just have more choices than before, we have more choices *per decision*. From what to wear to what to watch, we need more brain resources to decide the best, most confident selection. With this constant data-intensive decision-making activity, we experience *decision fatigue*.[6] This is the feeling of exhaustion at the end of a day when you haven't even broken a sweat. Your brain is tired, and you're out of mental resources. You're exhausted, unable to focus or process a coherent thought. You can't make good decisions, or maybe you are even unable to speak clearly or listen effectively. I call it being *spent*.

"...making decisions is hard work. First, you've got to weigh your options, which takes brain power. None of those decisions are necessarily overwhelming in and of themselves, but cumulatively

they take a toll and leave you increasingly exhausted as the day progresses. That's decision fatigue."

Source: Biohacking

Being Overinformed Causes Underconfidence

The opioid and suicide epidemics imply that life is truly challenging for many people. Social media undeniably beats down confidence and can cause clinical depression.[7] Plus, whether it is perceived to be fake or accurate news, we are inundated with extreme stories of sadness or success. From families separated by governments or tsunamis, to families flaunting their seemingly unearned fame and fortune, we can't help but wonder where we are in the social spectrum.

You already know that through every interpersonal exchange, whether online or in person, we only see and hear about other people's lives in highlighted moments. The anecdotes are spun to seem like normal everyday occurrences. Even though we realize that the posts are carefully curated, we still feel a fear of missing out (FOMO). We want the same attention, the same stuff, and the same seeming satisfaction to trigger other people's envy. We post and purchase to achieve what we think social success and satisfaction looks like.

Way back in 1940, Abraham Maslow explained that we all have a non-negotiable need to belong.[8] *(Read more about this in the section called, "It All Boils Down to Belonging.")* The internet now challenges us to constantly and quantitatively prove that we do. We value likes, shares, comments, and mentions, all to demonstrate that we matter.

Extrinsic Confidence Is Like a Carb

Someone boosting our confidence with a compliment or other validation may make us feel good temporarily, but it doesn't last, and may even make us feel emptier later. When we get this seemingly positive social feedback, it triggers a neurotransmitter in our brains called dopamine that makes us feel accomplished and confident.[9] When we don't get that social feedback enough, we behave like attention addicts who will do thoughtless, desperate things to feel good again.

I bet you know someone who is outright self-deprecating or always constantly self-doubting. How about someone who is perpetually dominating or unnecessarily defensive? Some people constantly check their phones for incoming messages, while others just don't stop talking.

We may even unknowingly harm other people in that hysterical craving to get our fix of emotional comfort. We overly brag about our connections or credentials to solicit someone's superficial respect. We inflate the fun or ease of something we've worked hard to accomplish or experience. We gloss over the complications or implications of the achievement so that we make it appear effortless and entitled. We do these stupid human internet tricks to seem perfect, special, even sovereign, while trying to hide our insecurity.

We may outright ask or casually solicit a sign from anyone who will offer to tell us that we are not alone, weird, or crazy. We crave views, likes, shares, comments, or any form of acceptance confirmation. Insanely, we allow a goofy emoji to control our confidence.

Another old social scientist, Pavlov,[10] comes to mind. Like dogs, we've been conditioned to seek reward, not from food, but from constant social validation. Unfortunately, we haven't made much progress in the last century. We have continued to 'dog' (slow down) and even prevent confidence in ourselves and our children, despite trying to be better parents than our own.

We Thought We Were Doing the Right Thing

Unfortunately, parenting is like fashion. It creates trendy styles that we look back at and wonder, *"What were we thinking?!?"*

Back in the 90's, experts encouraged parents to inspire self-esteem over competitiveness in children. Everyone should get a trophy, so there are only winners. Yet life doesn't follow that advice. Arguably, self-entitled millennials have high self-regard but perhaps the lowest resiliency. They aren't afraid to try new things but give up easily after failing. They typically lack patience and a persistent work ethic simply because they don't comprehend that some things must be learned and earned over time. They assume that there is always a hack, shortcut, or new tech that automates. With the inability to persevere and grow, both child and parent are often punished with a sense of failure and regret.

It is yet another generational example of how we tried to boost both parents' and children's confidence, but it backfired from a lack of accurate confidence understanding. Today, Tiger Moms still roar, and helicopter parents still hover. High-performance parents overschedule their kids with an exhausting agenda to increase a child's resumé and experiences. With no time left for children to think, teach, or talk at home, some schools are forced to add social-emotional learning as part of the already overloaded curriculum. We must better prepare ourselves and future generations for big data analysis. With or without silicon-assisted neural networks, we do complex critical thinking all day long using our own, organic neurology.

Our Brains Need Our Help

Our human need to belong and avoid confidence-crushing fears of failure and regret hasn't changed that much over time—nor has our mental resource quota. Yet, we want to consume a greater quantity of information, and we have more ways to get it and more ways it can be effectively doctored. We need to use a lot more brain cycles these days to perform critical thinking. Our executive function (as we'll discuss in the brain science chapter) has access to a finite pool of mental resources. These same resources also enable us to make confident decisions. There isn't an unlimited, on-demand supply despite the promise of energy drinks and health gurus. Sleep, good health, community, and continuous learning are the only proven ways so far that strengthen the human brain.[11] Plus, if the prefrontal cortex is not yet fully developed (which, on average, takes 25 years[12]), is damaged, or weakened from lack of use, it may be impossible for someone to create an intelligent thought, let alone a confident one.

Technology didn't create this escalating confidence crisis. It only made it easier and seemingly okay to fill our own confidence tank by taking it from other people online and otherwise. Every day, we steal confidence from other people and have some stolen from us, intentionally and not. It happens so commonly that we don't even register it as definitional bullying. We allow this socially acceptable behavior to erode how we feel about ourselves and other people – creating cynicism and disappointment. No wonder we are increasingly unhappy, disengaged, and frustrated.

Fit Wits

Charles Darwin[13] didn't anticipate Facebook or global competition. He could not predict that human survival of the fittest would need a lot more brains than brawn to adapt to modern day mental stress and neuronal shortage. Our reaction to combat this is to work harder, move faster, avoid reading, multitask, Google it up, drone and drop, grab and go. We can't survive without a cell signal. I have a feeling that Darwin would find this sociologically fascinating but equally sad.

Perhaps the seemingly new norm is all part of a grand social conspiracy to see who realizes that 24/7 distraction is a test, a phishing scheme, a way to eliminate the weak minded: *survival of the focused*. It makes for a great dystopian story except in our very real lives—too much choice is cognitive kryptonite and it is, no doubt, weakening everyone's confidence.

This confidence crisis begs us to accelerate human evolution. To do that, we need to sustainably make the one choice that you probably didn't know you could: *confidence.*

Defining Confidence

> *ACI's research found that it normally takes 60 years to reach our confidence best. So finally, there is a way to hack that—to dramatically shorten the process and get more control of our confidence and make it sustainably stronger. As a first step, we must define confidence and bring context to what we mean by self or personal confidence.*

When ACI asked 1,500+ people what confidence is, we received 1,500+ different answers. They ranged from "feeling comfortable in your skin," to "speaking your mind," to "having a good job." No doubt, confidence means different things to different people, in different circumstances, and at different times. What makes you confident today, may not make you feel that way tomorrow.

We also know from ACI research that confidence ebbs and flows with age, dipping dramatically at age 16 and finally peaking again at age 60. We realize that different things boost our confidence at different ages. We also found that while females self-report higher confidence initially, it plunges to half at age 16.[14] Male confidence levels typically stay more consistent throughout their life. Brain differences between genders is beyond the scope of this book and is still a hotly debated topic among researchers.

(See http://www.americanconfidenceinstitute.com/research-library/ for ACI's research summaries and related information.)

The Look of Confidence

As we set out to uncover what confidence really is, it helps to use our innate sense of what confidence looks like and how we naturally perceive it. We automatically detect confidence—or a lack thereof.

To prove this, I always ask keynote and workshop participants the following:

1. Identify a person you know now—or knew in the past—who you would consider confident. *(It shouldn't be a celebrity unless you know him/her personally.)*

---

2. Next, as precisely as possible, write down the things your selected person does that makes you recognize him/her as confident. How does he/she walk, talk, dress, stand, sit, smell, smile, etc.?

Don't just note that he/she owns the room – describe what they do when they walk in and how they act once in. How do they interact with other people? How do they carry themselves physically? What are the visible signs that the person is confident?

Consistent Confidence Characteristics

With over 50,000 respondents to date, the answers we hear are quite consistent. It is evident that we easily recognize and judge confidence in other people. We decide about someone's confidence immediately and that judgement impacts how we interact with and feel about that person.

Here is a summary list of what we most commonly hear. Confident people:

- Stay Calm—aren't jumpy or anxious
- Listen Better—pay attention actively
- Are decisive but diplomatic—don't waffle or ignore other people's input
- Don't judge—without enough data
- Appropriately apologize—don't say sorry unnecessarily

- Don't get defensive—don't blame other people or situations
- Are eager to learn—seek new knowledge and experiences

The last bullet, "eager to learn," is aligned with Carol Dweck's Growth Mindset body of work.[15] Perhaps no surprise, people who are open-minded and want to improve are better listeners and generally take in information more graciously. Dweck's research concludes that growth-minded individuals more often achieve success. Our dataset adds that these types of people are more confident, too.

You Can Fake News but Not Confidence

Being overall confident isn't a single behavior but a collection of consistent behaviors that someone executes without extrinsic motivation. Confident people don't need awards. They choose to be confident because it is a reward in itself.

Truly confident people aren't *acting* confidently, though they are *mirroring the behaviors* of confident role models. Confident people genuinely care about their impact on other people. Still, the hallmark of confident people is that they are comfortable with *who they are* and *what they do.*

Confident people stand up for what they truly believe with commitment and conviction. They don't waiver on decisions affecting their beliefs nor do they need others to follow. They want to have a positive interpersonal impact. Confident leaders won't sacrifice their values, unless they recognize it as necessary to support other people they value.

In this regard, confident people aren't always individuals you may like or agree with. Consider some politicians or relatives who may go against what you value, but you still consider them (definitionally) to be confident people. You may not like their manner or ideas, but you do respect their conviction and consistency.

Hopefully, you choose confident people who you admire as your own role models. They share and show the same values of the person you want to be, and they exemplify the way you also want to be known. Positive confidence role models "speak" to us much louder than words through their character, contributions, and habits.

Confident people don't give advice unless asked, they don't ever assume they are the best, and they try to override their inevitable biases so that they don't jump to conclusions. Nonetheless, they do make reasonably inclusive decisions and are notoriously humble. They own their errors and the responsibility to right them especially when the mistake impacts other people in any damaging way. They clearly care about other people's well-being, though they honor their own first.

The Confidence Trinity: Authenticity, Humility, and Trust

We hear so much these days about the importance of being authentic. Unfortunately, it is being used almost in contrast to having humility—being modest and humble about one's own individual importance. Arguably, humility is a higher-level requirement for confidence than authenticity or even honesty or compassion. Confidence is the fastest path to earn self and social trust.

Confident people love to learn—not to gain power—but because they are purely curious. Confidence gives them stability in life's many storms, so they can remain or quickly return to calmness despite stressful situations. Confident people are not always the "alpha" in the pack. They aren't necessarily leaders who take control, but they are the uniquely magnetic people in our world that keep us grounded and feeling safe.

Introverts May Actually Be More Confident

Many times, people will tell me they can't be confident because they are introverts. However, review the prior list of confidence characteristics to see that it demonstrates that introverts are more aligned with those traits. The necessary mindfulness of introverts suggests they have more mental control and conscientious responses.[16] Therefore, I surmise that introverts may be more likely to be confident than extroverts. A recent Predictive Index (PI) People Management Study[17] suggests that employees want leaders who are confident with traits most aligned to introversion. Introverts maintain the quiet, mindfulness required to listen, learn, and lead with grace and patience. One could argue that the brashness of some extroverts may be signs of overcompensating for a lack of confidence. Neither extroversion nor introversion determine confidence. They are different categories or lenses that describe personality and behavior.

Close but Not Quite—The Confidence Cousins

Like any type of fad, psychological trends often become popularized with socially conscious people. These novel explanations subsequently influence our parenting, teaching, and vocabulary. These "confidence cousins" are important parts of the confidence definition, but they are only subsets, ingredients, or aspects of confidence. Even together, they don't equal confidence.

Some examples of Confidence Cousins:

- **Self-Esteem**

Dictionary.com defines self-esteem as "a realistic respect for or favorable impression of oneself." From Dove[18] and L'Oréal commercials[19] to in-school assemblies, our society actively promotes feeling good about yourself just "because you're worth it." It is an unsubstantiated belief that you are awesome.

When proven that they really aren't as great as they believe they are, people with 'just' self-esteem often blame external factors for their own inability. They are unable to deal productively with the feelings of failure and may walk away from trying anything else in fear of future failure.

Self-esteem creates false pretenses about one's capabilities, and subsequently an inability to survive without the critical life skills of being resourceful and resilient. For example, giving children compliments about the beautiful picture they just drew turns out to be less helpful than constructively complimenting why you like it specifically. Recognizing *how* they did something rather than *what* they did allows them to apply the lessons to other circumstances. This equips them better to perform other related tasks—as well as cope and learn from failures.

- **Self-Compassion**

If you are self-compassionate, you accept that you are human and permit yourself to fail. This excuse helps you get back on the horse after being kicked off or falling off. Knowing how to "cut yourself some slack" is a critical life skill, if it isn't used as a cop-out for persisting past the mental or physical pain that often comes with growing and changing.

- **Self-Efficacy**

This is a belief that you can achieve a specific task or goal. It is a key component of confidence yet is also only a subset. Just because you *can* do something, doesn't mean you want to or should. Just because I know I can jump off a bridge, doesn't mean I am confident I'll do it well or am motivated to do it at all.

- **Courage**

When you have the confidence to say or do something, you have a surety about the most likely outcome. Courage, on the other hand, is being brave and accepting some potential pain despite not having all the information needed to be certain about the desired result. Courage tends to be temporal or situational. It may appear to be confidence in the absence of preparation.

- **Resilience**

Sometimes referred to having *grit*, resilient individuals seemingly don't let failure or challenge negatively impact their own lives. They appear to let things just roll off their back and move on. Not to be confused with indifference or ignorance, resilience helps you recover from setbacks. People who are resilient don't give up, and they don't let negative conditions or results become obstacles. Someone who is resilient doesn't fear failure but uses it as a lesson with the data about what to avoid doing next time. Some people embrace failure as obstinate or inspired motivation to try again.

One common way to be more resilient is to believe in a higher power or fate. Religion gives some people needed comfort and excuse by explaining the reason for why things happen(ed) beyond what they can explain as a result of their own actions. While I do not condone abdicating responsibility for your own behaviors, spiritual beliefs can enable some people to accept and move forward in an otherwise paralyzing situation. Therefore, if you consider that the *result* of faith gives believers resilience, that it's less about the way they obtained it, then the religious technique is no less honorable than just "manning up."

What Is NOT Confident

I use "not confident" because everyone is insecure in some areas of life. This isn't negative. Acknowledging personal weaknesses is an ultimate sign of confidence. It demonstrates surety about who you want to be, as well as who or what you do not.

It would seem likely that doing the same role model exercise as we did earlier to examine a confident person would yield the opposite answers about someone we know who is NOT confident. Yet, the list of common answers about non-confident characteristics yields many additional, clearly visible, behavioral tells:

- Avoiding eye contact—looking anywhere except at the other person's eyes
- Slouching—shoulders are concave or rounded inward

- Nervous giggling—laughing when something isn't truly funny
- Constantly seeking approval—asking for confirmation of opinion or fact heard in a vocal uptick, or outright question of agreement
- Physical ticks/fidgeting—any type of nervous action such as nail biting or twitching
- Speaking in a very quiet or loud voice—someone who desperately does or does not want to be heard
- Interrupting—constantly taking over a conversation
- Always disagreeing—especially if the person agrees but just likes to be contentious.

"Not confident" behaviors can show up occasionally for everyone but are more often hallmarks of people with overall weak confidence. I have some clearly brilliant friends who frequently show signs of insecurity such as rubbing their earlobes, twitching their shoulders, or avoiding eye contact. While I respect their ideas and friendship, I also recognize these habits are signs that their confidence is being challenged. This doesn't make me dislike or respect these friends less; it just saddens me that they aren't able to control their superpower. I want to help them overcome whatever is causing them to worry. Yet, I also know that unsolicited help like that can be the worst thing you can do when an otherwise strongminded person is, in that instance, lacking confidence.

Confidence Imposters

We all know and interact with people who display behaviors which ACI calls the "Confidence Imposters." These are dominant personalities or habitual behaviors that can fake us out. Someone displaying these behaviors wants others to think he/she is confident, even though he/she most likely knows inside that they are not.

These are different than just "not confident" behaviors. The reason ACI calls them imposters is that when we come into contact with and clearly identify an Imposter, we recognize the "not confident" behavior but simultaneously *question our own judgement* about the person. We second-guess our own confidence about the imposter ("Maybe they are as cool as they think they are. Maybe I am misjudging and am the one who is wrong."). Thus, imposter behavior is manipulative, though often unintentionally.

Confidence Imposter examples include someone who is always:

- **Cocky/Bitchy**. Sometimes perceived as overconfident, the difference here is that cocky/bitchy people act this way because they want other people to feel inferior. Overconfident people tend to have inflated, and typically ignorant, high self-regard.

- **Bitter/Cynical**. You can recognize these behaviors from the sour puss or as I call them, *pucker faces*—people with drawn in cheeks who always respond "no." They are always negative and suck the energy and optimism out of everyone. Toxic and controlling, these behaviors are clear indicators that someone lacks confidence.

- **Demanding**. These people are bossy or simply don't care about other people's input or needs.

- **Pedantic/Condescending**. Someone that talks down to, or overly simplistically to, other people so the other people feel stupid and small.

- **Disingenuous**. This is when someone deliberately pretends to know less than they do to *fake out* or *egg on* another person. It is a derivative of pedantic, condescending behavior.

- **Commentating**. Someone who always adds their two cents even when it is not helpful, requested, or otherwise relevant.

- **Disagreeable**. Some people just have a habit of disagreeing—or else they find pleasure in it as a sinister sport. The disagreeing person enjoys debating, even if they don't really believe in the side they are supporting. It is a derivative of Smartest Person in the Room (discussed more under Bonehead Behaviors) with a motivation to be disruptive. It is another method of controlling a conversation and taking confidence from other people. Being a Devil's Advocate can be helpful if it is done constructively to tighten the other person's confidence. But when someone habitually disagrees, their intention is to loosen another's confidence.

- **Naysaying**. A naysayer is someone who raises a problem or concern without ever seeing positive parts or offering better solutions. Sometimes this is a form of habitually disagreeing. Naysayers are automatically negative about everything—whether they do or do not agree with the presented idea.

Liar, Liar, Confidence on Fire

While we aren't born with a confidence gene, we do all have an intuitive 6th sense—we know a faker when we see one. We can smell fake people a mile away even without talking to them. We recognize the body language, typically more than their usually carefully crafted words. Our "Spidey-sense" alerts us that something is not right with the faker's behavior and to beware of the faker's true intentions.

When we do sense a lack of someone else's confidence, we make our own decision about how to respond. We may feel sorry for him/her but subsequently not alter our own behaviors. Unfortunately, when someone is faking it, we may then second guess our detection. We wonder if we are misreading or misjudging whether their seemingly fake confidence is real confidence. We question OUR confidence about THEIR confidence.

We may even tolerate imposter behavior, but we still don't like it. We smell fraud and therefore don't trust imposters. We may feel sorry for them and perhaps angry that they try to manipulate us. We know them as grandstanding and self-centered individuals, often toxic. Yet we often let them into our heads where they rattle our confidence.

Recognizing these types of people in the future, you can be assured that they are "not confident" or even overconfident. Next time put up your confidence shield to deflect some of their behaviors, so they don't impact your own.

Now that you have some ideas about what confidence looks like and doesn't, we can present a precise definition of what it is.

Truth and Confidence

If you look at any online or paper-based dictionary for the word confidence, the most common definition is:

"Confidence is the certainty about the truth of something."

This certainty subsequently drives our thoughts, decisions, and behaviors.

If I ask you if you are confident that the weather will stay the same tomorrow, you will consider the current weather forecasts that you may have heard, maybe a recent read of the almanac, or even the position of the moon. You might even consider other less public information such as how your joints feel or how your hair looks. You'll take into consideration the overall accessible information, as well as the ramifications of being incorrect. Then you'll state whether you are confident that the weather will remain the same. You will also then decide how to dress, drive, or otherwise act accordingly.

If I asked you to comment on the next political election, a potential investment, or any other opinion-based topic, you would use a similar process of available data collection and analysis in your head. You may request additional time to collect more information and to think through your answer. The same process would, in fact, apply to any decision. You would 1) collect information; 2) analyze and maybe repeat steps 1 and 2; and, 3) decide what you believe to be true. If you have *enough* information, experience, analysis, etc., you will state your answer *with confidence*. And yes, you can also be confident that you are not confident.

You may be familiar with the term *consumer confidence*, which is a way to predict the future health of the economy. Economists measure how much a sample set of people are reflecting confidence that their future paychecks will continue to arrive. When people are sure that they have/will have spending power, they can pay for non-essential purchases they make. Thus, when consumer confidence is high, the short-term economic outlook is deemed positive. In a mind-bending way, the paycheck confidence of consumers fuels their confidence to shop, which in turn fuels economists to confidently predict a confident future economy. (See how confidence affects everything?!)

Even scientific or other measurable disciplines factor in confidence when stating results or quantitative facts. They seek an acceptable level of certainty (within expected potential deviation) that buffers the fact that their conclusion is as confident (true) as possible.

At its core, confidence is a decision—it is whether you are certain enough about something to believe, pass an opinion, state a fact, act upon, or otherwise accept it as true. With that certainty, you *decide* or *determine* whether you are confident. We misleadingly say that we *feel* confident as a result of making thoughtful decisions. Confidence isn't a state or feeling. It is the process and result of reaching a *certain enough* decision.

Self—or Better Yet—Personal Confidence

It's one thing to measure your certainty about something like the weather or the stock market. It's another to ask if you feel confident as a person. Since ACI contends that confident people care about their *impact* on other people, we refrain from the phrase "self-confidence" as it is too haughty and otherwise self-centered. We use "Personal Confidence" instead, and after thousands of hours of research, thinking and discussions, our definition is thus:

"Personal Confidence is being certain enough about the truth of your values, needs, and wants that in turn drive your thoughts, decisions, and behaviors."

That is, when you are clear about WHO you want to be—not *what*—you can then choose to act, react, and interact with confidence. When you are certain *enough* about your chosen path and boundaries, you can behave in a fearless way within your self-defined success. Moreover, you decide what is right for *you* without dependence on other people's rules.

To achieve this, it requires clarity about your values and honest self-awareness about how those values are—or are not—reflected in your behaviors. If you say you want to be known as a generous person but rarely give anything, it creates mental misalignment (aka cognitive dissonance) in your head and everyone else's. If you give away things all the time but do it for no other reason than you want people to like you, you may be trying to compensate for your insecurity. Alternatively, a confident person who values generosity willingly gives to others because they want to be known as someone who is generous. Some would say there is no such thing as true altruism because we are all motivated by self-interests. Whether that is true or not, confident people are motivated to live according to their values. They confidently decide what is right for them and act accordingly. This may mean consciously suspending some of their personal values at times, to honor a valued group's need. The key is making the decision conscientiously to respect what you are certain that you value, need, and want.

There is a subtle but VERY CRITICAL point in the confidence definition that must be addressed:

You Are Never 100% Certain

Nothing is that absolute. As stated before, even with scientific confidence, there is always some small and acceptable level of possible incorrectness. There may be information that you may not know or have misinterpreted. Therefore, personal confidence is a relative measure when you are certain ENOUGH that you are more likely right than wrong, more likely to succeed than fail, more likely to be able than not—*at that time, given that situation.*

Consider overall confidence like a balance-based weight scale. When your opinion has enough informational weight tipping in your favor, then you are confident. Unfortunately, perfection can drag down progress and cause missed opportunities. For many people (especially women), they are only confident when the scale is completely tipped. They will act only with absolute certainty that every "i" and "t" are done perfectly. A still often-quoted 2014 Harvard Study[20] found that on average, women only apply to roles when they are 100% certain they can meet the job requirements, as compared to men who apply with only a 60% match. Even if you don't agree with the study yourself, we should all use the word *enough* a lot more often to allow ourselves to be a "minimal viable person." We forget that we are often *good enough* when compared to everyone else who is also self-assessing and obsessing.

Certain enough requires an acceptance of realistic benchmarks and expectations. It requires us to see ourselves accurately with self-compassion relative to everyone else with the same flaws and challenges. One of the most powerful things you can do to be more confident is reexamine your self-defined standards of "enough." I bet you are a better person than you give yourself credit for.

Hacking Confidence

Having clarity about who you want to be is typically a long and character-building process. That is why it takes most people 60 years to become fully confident. By that time, we finally learn what is important to us and what isn't—including not caring about what other people think about us! It takes us a lifetime to finally free ourselves from seeing ourselves through other people's eyes. Only then do we put our time, energy, and money into the things that fit with certainty into our values, needs, and wants. We can then finally live as our most confident selves (unfortunately within the limits of our worn bodies).

If you're 60 or older, you're probably laughing with satisfied confirmation like every one of the 60+ year old people we interviewed. If you're not yet 60, the great news is you're ahead of the confidence curve! By just reading this book, you're already hacking the confidence process to have much more time and energy to live a more confident life.

Part 2: CALIBRATE

Calculating Confidence

> *The world seemingly does not need another assessment since there are already hundreds of others that ascertain behavioral, emotional, and intellectual ability. Assessments can help determine someone's job fit, learning style, or coachability. All have a similar goal to at least increase self-awareness. Some aim to identify and/or change behavior. Yet, despite all the other assessments out there, we felt compelled by the constant requests ACI received to develop a way to measure and monitor confidence.*

We're Addicted to Data

We seek to measure and analyze almost everything these days. We now have tools and technology that enable us to capture and compute massive amounts of data to identify patterns and proof.

Data scientists are some of the highest earners and most sought-out professionals. However, you will find amateur data wonks in every profession—searching for some type of data to justify a proposal, idea, or decision. Data gives us comfort because it quells emotions. As you will learn soon in this book, analyzing data allows the rational, calmer, and confident part of our brain to be in control so we feel more comfortable with our decision. Also, despite a gut or intuitive opinion, we often let data drive decisions because it is easier to lean on and blame the data if things go wrong. We analyze data to make relatively simple decisions such as what to wear on any given day. We might factor in the weather report or simply look at the sky. Bigger, more costly decisions such as deciding if the weather is okay to launch a space missile, require us to gather and analyze a greater amount of, and more complex, data.

When we do have *enough* quality data, it provides us with defendable rationalization so we can make confident decisions. Data helps us be objective and removes baked-in biases. Especially when we need to assess something relatively subjective like human performance, data helps normalize political perspectives and ego-driven end games. Thus, we demand data and may also contest it when the process feels potentially tainted. Think about any decision you didn't agree with or didn't like: an election, an award, a performance review, or a reorg. We use data to justify decisions, especially difficult or group ones. The data's accuracy and application also need to stand up to naysayer scrutiny. Therefore, having data can help or hurt confidence depending on many decision-making factors. It can substantiate as well as discriminate. Data can provide evidence, but it can also mask root problems. Ideally, data facilitates thinking and invites dialogue, which can be very helpful—even in the absence of absolute answers.

For decades now, the Intelligence Quotient (IQ) test has been used to estimate intelligence. More recently, Emotional Intelligence (EQ) has caught on in almost every field. Both measurements have their share of pundits and fans since any assessment is going to be challenged for its uncomfortable insights and inevitable shortcomings. Nonetheless, these and other assessments remain in use to help teachers, managers, coaches, and others determine human achievement and potential. Ideally, the data is used to decide on better individualized learning needs. Assessments, for better or worse, are also applied to predict job placement and performance as well as to help manage disabilities and medical needs.

All assessments have a base assumption that a person's results are either fixed over time, or not. For example, an individual's personality assessment should not change over time. Behavioral assessments vary—some declare you are what you are and do what you do. Others aim to help change behavior. Assessments also vary in the testing technique and use of resulting data. Some assessments require an expert to interpret results and recommend next steps. Other assessments provide the individual with his/her own set of result-determined recommendations.

Myers-Briggs,[21] DISC,[22] and Predictive Index[23] are examples of formal assessments that have been used by all types of professional organizations for decades. Cosmopolitan Magazine is well known for its quick and saucy assessments. Even your zodiac or horoscope can be used as a self-awareness tool—anything that provides personal and/or interpersonal feedback for you to contemplate. What you do with the feedback is the real question. The information should help you be a better version of who you want to be.

The Missing Measurement

In my many confidence-related interactions with people from all walks of life, I am constantly asked how to measure confidence. The head of a large angel investment firm asked me to develop an entrepreneurial confidence measurement tool. He said that confidence was a key metric his firm was looking for in the entrepreneurs in whom the firm would considering investing. Confidence enables entrepreneurs to weather the inevitable startup storms and potential pivots. Confidence is an indicator of coachability and open mindedness—both important entrepreneurial virtues to all types of investors. Confident entrepreneurs, unlike arrogant or insecure ones, make better leaders. Whether they are pitching to prospective customers, employees, partners, or future investors, entrepreneurs need authentic confidence to sell confidence to everyone else.

The problem is that entrepreneurial confidence isn't something you can see in a written business plan or slide deck. These days, everyone uses online templates so the documents all pretty much look the same. Investors can only assess an entrepreneur's confidence by taking the time to meet with him/her. If I could hack that process, I was told it would be an angel to the angels.

Other people have asked me for a confidence diagnostic to help them better manage their employees and kids. Essentially such an assessment would replace an uncomfortable conversation and enable data-driven self-help. Recruiters have asked ACI to help sift out confident candidates from those who have misleadingly impressive resumes. Business/life/personal coaches and mentors have also asked for such support to shortcut and justify their work with their clients. Academics have asked for such a tool to lend proof that their schools obtain relevant results beyond job placement rates.

In response to these requests, ACI developed various models, systems, and partnerships culminating with the 2020 release of an exciting confidence assessment tool.

The Confidence Quotient (CQ)

The overall intention of the Confidence Quotient (CQ) Assessment is to help individuals be more aware of the subconscious or Root Source Thoughts that drive or deter their confidence. CQ can serve as a benchmarking and monitoring tool to prove progress of one's own *confidence journey*. By validating progress, it also gives users the confidence that they are strengthening their confidence.

The Confidence Quotient was developed in partnership with Think X,[24] a company that has been successfully doing Root Thought assessment for over 30 years. Root Source Thoughts are planted as a result of life experiences and learnings. They contribute to mindsets and subsequently to attitudes and behaviors. Root Source Thinking is subconscious and directs the rest of your thinking. Root Source Thinking creates or activates neural pathways that become your automatic mindsets and beliefs. Identifying Root Thoughts and their associated undesirable behavior allows us to build new pathways that 'reroute' thinking to achieve more desired behaviors.

For example:

> **Root Source Thinking**: I am not smart enough.
> **Belief**: I am not a success.
> **Internal Dialogue**: I can't..., I tried and failed..., I am a failure.
> **Mindset**: Fixed/Self-Deprecating
> **Behavioral Impact**: A lack of risk-taking or inability to apply total effort/potential.

As opposed to:

> **Root Source Thinking**: My life's success or failure is up to me.
> **Belief**: I am a success.
> **Internal Dialogue**: I can do what I put my mind to, no matter what.
> **Mindset**: Growth/Independent/Responsible
> **Behavioral Impact**: Positive outlook with an eagerness to try/learn new things and resilience to achieve.

A Situational Assessment, Not a One and Done Test

CQ can help identify both simple and complex thinking that can be changed to improve confidence, though none of these are immediate, effortless fixes. Any mindset, habit, or behavior change needs to be practiced so it eventually becomes a hardwired neural, automatic response.

Whether you work on your own or with a coach, CQ gives you a more targeted, and therefore faster, result. Your customized CQ Report includes a short analysis of your overall and individual driver scores, as well as associated coaching tips.

For example, depending on your scores, you might be advised to work on being a more active listener or find strategies to more calmly take on new tasks. By just doing a CQ, you gain confidence with this insightful, data-driven first step.

Also note that the Confident Quotient (CQ) is not a static rating, but rather a way to assess your Root Source Thinking and subsequent confidence drivers and obstacles. You might take the assessment a day, week, or year later and find you have a different score. Circumstance, experience, mood, climate, and hundreds of other factors may impact your results. You will not create new Root Source Thinking and subsequent changed habits and behaviors until you consciously desire to and do something proactively to change them.

Find Out Your CQ

The CQ Assessment is only available using our highly secure, online system. Once completed, your personal report is emailed directly to you.

You can use the resulting information on your own or share it with a trusted confidant such as a coach, mentor, or manager. If you don't have your own confidant, ACI is happy to match your requirements to one of our excellent Certified Confidence Coaches.

Take the Confidence Quotient (CQ) Assessment at:

http://www.americanconfidenceinstitute.com/CQ

(Note: There is a cost to take the CQ Assessment, though it is included in some of ACI's online programs. CQ bundles are also available for coaches or individuals who want to purchase more than one assessment at a time.)

Confidence Brain Science Made Simple

> *You may be intimidated and therefore inclined to skip this chapter, but don't do it! Your brain is your body's command center, so once you know how it works, you can better operate it—as well as other people's! Plus, pushing your brain to do and learn new things helps it to function better overall.*

As I taught both of my sons to drive, they needed a general idea of how a car works. They didn't really need to know about pistons, valves, hoses, etc. to drive under *normal* conditions. Yet, when New England roads get icy, it helps them to know more about torque and braking systems, among other functional details that help them to make better driving decisions.

While we all drive our brains day-to-day without really knowing what is under the "hoodie," with a bit more knowledge about the brain, we can drive our own—and other people's—behaviors better, especially in challenging conditions.

A Better Brain Without Pain

Brain Science is a superset of neurology, psychology, and social science. It encompasses multidisciplinary research, technology, and techniques used to study, treat, and improve the brain. There are many motivations to better understand our brains, including more effective ways to repair and strengthen them. Researchers seek to augment deficient brains with medical devices surgically implanted or externally connected. There are a plethora of ingested or injected pharmacological solutions. Some experts use non-invasive brainwave monitoring and other biofeedback measurement to enable patients to have more mental control. Plus, some brain scientists seek to understand why existing mind-body practices such as mindfulness, physical/movement therapies, memory exercises, visioning, etc. can also help cognitive function.

Yoga, meditation, martial arts, and other Eastern mind/body practices have been used by so many people around the world for thousands of years. If they didn't work for at least some people, these techniques would not have persisted. Yet, only now do we have the technology—including Functional Magnetic Resonance Imaging (fMRI)—that can help examine an active brain to *know* why these age-old techniques work. We know there is untapped power in our brains to have much more control over our bodies and behaviors. While it varies between people and depending on circumstances, we can control mindset and attitude, habits and confidence.

While the brain has many functions and regions, we will focus on four key cognitive ones that are the most involved with confident thoughts, decisions, and resulting behaviors.

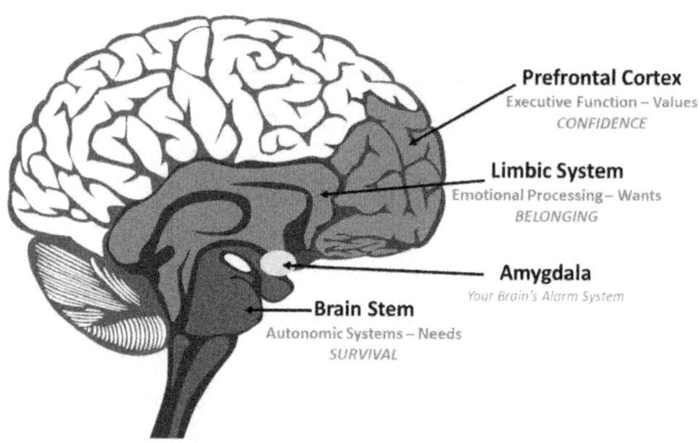

The Old But Not So Wise Brain Stem

The bottom region is the BRAIN STEM. It is in the back of your head and connects to your spinal cord and central nervous system. The Brain Stem is responsible for all your autonomic* functions—the ones you don't really "think" about doing such as breathing, sweating, heartbeat, etc.—essentially the body functions that you **need** for survival.

*Something that is **automatic** can operate without external control or intervention while something **autonomic** is acting or occurring involuntarily, without conscious control.[25]*

The Brain Stem is the oldest part of the human brain and was the most prominent part of the cavepeople's brains. It enabled them to perform the necessary, and luckily limited, decision-making needed to survive back then. For example, they would decide to run towards the wild boar to capture it for dinner—or—they would decide to run away so *they* didn't become *its* dinner.

This now well-known "fight or flight" response is largely managed in the Brain Stem, which makes an unconscious, reactionary decision about whether to attack or to retreat. A more relatable example would be if you accidentally drop a knife, you will instinctually move your foot out of the way. That is the brain stem in control. You don't really think about moving your foot. Your Brain Stem reacts (flight) almost immediately upon receiving the urgent internal alarm: "move foot, knife falling!"

This fast-path, neural messaging is your brain's emergency management system. It can save you in times of great danger by essentially taking over when you don't have time to think. However, because the Brain Stem reacts automatically, it can cause you to react rashly and sometimes regretfully. Fist fights are largely the Brain Stem's fault. When you are uncontrollably nervous, anxious, or otherwise sweating, palpitating, or hyperventilating, your Brain Stem again can mostly be blamed.

The Brain Stem takes over and can turn up many of your body functions with neurotransmitters such as energy-enabling adrenaline and stress-inducing cortisol. With these natural neuro-stimulators, your body is revved up and ready to fight or flee. Your Brain Stem protects you by taking immediate, and essentially *thoughtless* action. While the Brain Stem is motivated to keep you physically and emotionally safe, a knee jerk reaction may later come at a physical or emotional cost.

Little Shop of Wants & Worries

While emotions are created by all sorts of experiences, memories, smells, sights, and other data inputs into different parts of your brain, the LIMBIC SYSTEM is most recognized as your emotional HQ. Whenever you are experiencing love, hate, anger, sadness, happiness, or other feelings, these emotions are ruminating in your Limbic System, which drives behaviors that reflect what you **want**.

Because memories are managed by another part of the brain located close to the Limbic System, you can appreciate that our memories have a great impact on our emotions. (FYI—emotions can also change memories.[26]) That is why you often remember events more clearly if you had an emotional experience at that time. You might not easily remember what you had for breakfast, but you can probably recall every detail of when you learned about the 9/11 attacks or the details of your first romantic kiss. The emotional tie creates what is called a *flashbulb memory* that memorializes the picture (actually the *perceived* picture—sometimes even your brain's *preferred* picture) in your mind.[27] You clearly remember those experiences because your Limbic System burned the emotionally-charged memory into your brain.

To understand how your Limbic System functions, think of it as an emotional kitchen. It takes a variety of information (ingredients) from current situations and experiences. It draws from sources including your memories, your senses (taste, smell, touch, sight, hearing), your physical state, and other circumstantial factors to create the resulting emotional dish that is then served to the rest of your brain. The emotional dish then gets consumed and judged differently by the different parts of your brain. For example, when you are frustrated, your Brain Stem may take that and create aggressive behavior and subsequently make your face red or cause you to cry. Your heart rate may increase, and your muscles may tense. Frustration can be 'tasted' differently by your more rational responses, using that food to fuel persistence or reevaluation.

The Limbic System on its own doesn't really decide how you behave—it creates neural data about the thoughts it has at that moment, or any associated from an experience. The resulting emotional data triggers (activates) neural pathways that cause us to feel and behave in accordance. When seeing a sad movie, your Limbic System may trigger you to cry. Watch a comedy and you'll laugh and smile. Feel anxious about giving a presentation and you may be terrified or excited by the opportunity.

A neuroeconomic study found that people even invest money more freely when their favored sports team is winning.[28] Why? Because our emotions stimulate neurotransmitters and hormones that drive behaviors. Strong emotional experiences can therefore also activate behavioral responses just by remembering them, long after the experience. A smell or sight might trigger a memory and subsequent action. For example, whenever I walk into an old NY apartment building and smell old world cooking, I have an insatiable desire to make my grandmother's brisket.

What makes this all so complex is that emotions are triggered by neural-stimulations, which trigger behaviors, but it can work in reverse too—meaning, behaviors can stimulate emotions. When you are charitable, you feel proud or lucky. When you work out, you feel accomplished and peaceful. All of these can be explained by neurotransmission activation. Suffice it to say in our brief exploration, that the Limbic System is key to managing emotions and triggering subsequent behavior.

This is all part of human biology and evolution which is often out of our immediate or direct control. However, by using the emotional data more consciously, we can build mental strength, agility, and resilience. We can also choose to be confident.

For a much more in-depth explanation, I highly suggest "How Emotions Are Made: The Secret Life of the Brain" by Lisa Feldman Barrett Ph.D. or anything by Dr. Robert Sapolsky.

Your Own CEO: The Prefrontal Cortex

You can think about the Brain Stem as the Chief Operations Officer (COO) that keeps your main systems running smoothly. Your Limbic System can be thought of as the Chief Marketing Officer (CMO) which creates moods and perceptions, wants and worries. Carrying this metaphor forward, these and other parts of your brain are subordinated to the Chief Executive Officer (CEO): The PREFRONTAL CORTEX. Here, executive functions enable us to manage, organize, prioritize, value, analyze, rationalize, consider, calculate, and intellectualize. Essentially, all our rational thinking and decision-making happen in the Prefrontal Cortex.

When the Prefrontal Cortex is strong and effective, it takes in and assimilates different types of information—objective and subjective data coming from the outside world—as well as inside your head from memories, biases, and other existing thoughts. It analyzes all this available data to decide which part of the brain will activate the appropriate behaviors and physical responses.

My neuroscience superhero, Dr. Robert Sapolsky, often says the Prefrontal Cortex makes us do the harder things.[29] This means doing things that are challenging, scary, against habit, or contrary to learned appropriateness. When our Limbic System doesn't *want* to do something, our Prefrontal Cortex can help consider the potential outcomes of doing or not doing that uncomfortable thing. It weighs the pros and cons as well as the potential implications. This computation may happen consciously or not. Our Prefrontal Cortex helps us overcome mental gravitational pull to the lower, less proactive, protective, and often lazier parts of the brain. When we decide we are confident, it is because the Prefrontal Cortex has decided it is so.

The Prefrontal Cortex is in the front of your head, protected by your skeletal forehead. It is the part of the brain that makes us uniquely human and of all animals, we have the largest, most sophisticated Prefrontal Cortex. Cavepeople didn't have this full advantage and it is the newest part of the human brain to fully evolve. Today, as humans develop from babies to adults, the Prefrontal Cortex is still the last part of the brain to develop, not fully forming until we reach, on average, age 25.[30] *(Ah ha! Now you know why teenagers make such emotional and seemingly irrational decisions. They don't have the brain matter needed to totally think rationally yet.[31])*

Consider that babies and kids grow this part of their brains while they are learning all things human—how to walk, talk, reach, run, play, write, etc. They are training their brains at an incredible pace but simply do not have the brain structures in place—yet—to effectively determine consequences, correlate data, or identify personal values.

We need our Prefrontal Cortex to not only know what we value, but to recognize when something is not aligned with our values. No wonder so many of us pick careers at a pre-prefrontal age and then figure out later in our lives that even if we are good at the job, we just don't like or value it.

Chief of Staff – The Amygdala

A small, but very powerful part of the brain is called the AMYGDALA. It's the size of an almond and sits above the Brain Stem, tucked low in the Limbic System. The Amygdala is always on the lookout for incoming physical or emotional danger. I like to compare it to a Chief of Staff because it is usually the first part of your brain to be notified of incoming information and subsequently triages it to another part of your brain.

In the previous example of dropping a knife accidentally, your Amygdala instantly sends an alarm to your brain that something dangerous is potentially happening. The proximity of the Amygdala to the Brain Stem is no evolutionary accident. In an emergency such as a dropped knife, the Amygdala uses a literally named *fast neural pathway* to the Brain Stem next door which immediately moves your foot away to avoid being stabbed.

For situations that aren't quite as dire, the Amygdala can choose to use a slower—though still split second—neural pathway to warn other cognitive parts of the brain and trigger action. For example, when you are worried about failing a test, the Amygdala may choose to send the alarm to the Brain Stem OR to the Prefrontal Cortex. You will react differently depending on which direction the alarm is sent. If it is sent down to the Brain Stem, you may get anxious, be unable to sleep, and have an increased heart rate. You may not be able to focus and instead, you may start sweating and/or have a full-on panic attack.

If the alarm is sent upstairs to the Prefrontal Cortex, you can think and decide what to do more consciously. You might rationalize that it's only one test out of many, recall that you are well prepared, and/or maybe you remind yourself to use deep breathing or another stress management technique. When you keep the Prefrontal Cortex in charge, you can better think and cope before, during, and after the test.

It is seemingly easier to let the emergency alarm fall to the Brain Stem. It is not the fault of gravity but rather a lack of mental strength, practice, and acquired skill needed to send the alarm up into the Prefrontal Cortex. This brain control is what ACI calls *Metaconfident Thinking*. We will discuss this more in detail later but for now, just know that when we realize that we *can* make a choice, we can consciously control *how* we think and therefore, *how* we want to behave.

Bicycle Brain

In normal, expected conditions, you can drive your brain like coasting along smooth pavement on a bicycle. You still need to pay attention and work a little to stay balanced, but the bicycle moves forward, and your body/behavior intuitively goes along for the ride.

Then life happens.

You hit a pebble, such as a difficult colleague or being asked to do something unknown. Maybe you are passed over for a promotion, a raise, or don't get a job you really thought was a slam dunk. Other things such as being laid off, not winning something you trained hard for, a surprisingly bad performance review, or other personal disappointments are all frustrating, costly setbacks—but not life threatening or permanently debilitating situations. Maybe you are faced with something even more disruptive akin to hitting a rock which causes you to either fall or jump off the bicycle. When you or someone you care about gets sick, it is more than a speed bump— your life comes to a screeching halt at least temporarily. You eventually navigate past the rock and continue your way forward, maybe a bit bruised, but at least more aware and watchful. Maybe forever after, you go a little slower or wear protective padding.

Inevitably, you may hit a wall—a divorce, death of a loved one, or other life crisis that knocks you off your path so hard that the memorable pain may stop you from wanting to get back on your bicycle again. Even if you decide to move forward, you may move cautiously slow with a cynical attitude. You know that you were damaged and don't want to be hurt again. The fear makes you uber-vigilant, worried that you won't survive another fall. It holds you back from taking risks or trying to do anything similar.

The additional mental overhead is exhausting and reduces the cognitive resources available for you to apply otherwise. Trauma doesn't just temporarily kick confidence. Trauma taints how we perceive potential danger and behave forever after. Unpredictably, the trauma can be like a planted landmine in our brains ready to explode at any future moment retriggering the fear and causing us to relive the emotional pain.

Any type of traumatic experience can damage positive, desired neural pathways. Trauma can also create new negative, undesired ones. Trauma is typically associated with external circumstances that are physically or emotionally negatively impactful.

Understandably experiences such as a concussion, a death of a loved one, or any form of physical abuse can cause emotional trauma.

You can be traumatized any time your feelings are 'hurt' or if you feel that you just aren't good enough to succeed or don't fit in. Emotional trauma, in fact, can happen from anything that we 'decide' isn't socially acceptable. We all have different thresholds or tolerances for what makes something just unfortunate, versus something that is stressfully traumatic. For example, if you experienced your parents going through an ugly divorce, it will likely affect how you view marriage and how you may behave within one. Any type of rejection from a relationship, job, or college application will put that experience into your neural database. As a result, even years later, you may be leery about applying for other opportunities because you consciously or subconsciously want to avoid that same feeling of rejection.

Whether your perception of the past failure, regret, or rejection is accurate or not, the feelings can cause real and lasting trauma. A welcomed learning opportunity for some, can be a lifelong, confidence-crushing challenge for others. For example, my nephew loves taking tests because he enjoys the challenge and he has tested successfully most of his life. On the other hand, my son, who is the same age, gets anxious every time he has to take a test because he remembers all the negative test experiences he's had. Do both boys go into tests with the same starting block to succeed? Clearly not. My son is learning to overcome his self-defeat based on past performances. My other son, a tennis player, has been taught that every point matters and that past performance isn't an indicator of success, if you are confidently prepared and are still motivated to win. I'm sure you can imagine the dinner table conversations in my house!

Therefore, the ubiquitous psychological question is can we overcome a traumatic rock/setback when it leaves a cognitive scar?

Traumatic experiences are burned into memory, so any similar situation immediately gets flagged to remind us of the potential danger. Unless we consciously intervene in the reaction decision, our Brain Stem will take over to protect us from the new, perceived potential danger. Poking a lion or having your Amygdala poked by trauma have the same result: fierce defensiveness. People who need to overcome (better manage) any type of traumas are typically helped via therapeutic awareness and strategies. Overcoming trauma requires much more expertise than the scope of this book and may require medical intervention. Within our continued discussion here, we are focused on typical confidence-kicking—but no less lousy—traumas. And while we can't control all the confidence-compromising traumas life throws at us, we can more consciously control our own decisions about how we want to respond.

Approaching confidence-challenging situations isn't simply a matter of having a positive situational or general mindset. We behave according to our own neural pathways which get formed and changed from our knowledge and experiences – good and bad, minor and traumatic.

This is simply part of being human. We all experience pebbles, rocks, and walls which can hurt us. How well we recover and learn from these experiences not only adds to our character, but it defines how we choose to live. This is where your confidence truly is tested and can matter the most.

Confidence enables us to eventually decide to not go, go in a different direction, and/or use different means to get where we want to go. It is not that the brain doesn't fear being hurt again. Rather, the Prefrontal Cortex consciously weighs potential outcomes. It considers that NOT moving forward could have a negative impact that hurts us as much as running into another potential wall. Confident people don't let fear dictate their decisions—they choose to use fear as relevant information, not justification for immobilization. They may decide to avoid a situation but only after they confidently decide it is the best course of action.

When the Amygdala perceives physical or emotional danger, it needs to decide which part of the brain it will warn and trigger action. Sometimes it is evident which part is better-suited. When someone cuts you off driving on the highway, your Amygdala screams to the Brain Stem to immediately swerve you to safety (and may cause you to reflectively shout or signal a profanity to the reckless driver, too).

Depending on the type of danger, it is not always clear which part of the brain should take control. Some potential physical dangers, such as a decision to skydive, can be carefully contemplated, but you don't have time to invoke the Prefrontal Cortex after accidentally dropping a knife. When there is emotional danger, there is always time to think and choose which part of our brain should manage the situation.

However, we don't usually know that we *can* and that we *should* do this. And while it is not always easy or automatic, confident people consciously take time to think. They don't react until their Prefrontal Cortex is ready. They know to pause and ponder before acting, reacting, or interacting. This seemingly simple act of control allows them to consult their values, needs, and wants so they ensure their behaviors are within those guidelines.

The objective is to preempt an Amygdala moment when your confidence may be compromised. If you can catch the warning, you can proactively push the notification up to your Prefrontal Cortex so you can think calmly and respond confidently. This is not so much a hijacking, but rather a superadmin role. You consciously/mindfully/deliberately take control of your thinking so you can better decide and drive your behaviors.

To build this skill, you first need to recognize the main emotional dangers that trigger an Amygdala alarm.

While there are infinite types of potential emotional dangers, the three big ones that impact confidence are:

1) the fear of **failure**

2) the fear of **regret**

3) the fear of **rejection**

As humans, most of us do not want to risk failing, especially when we don't foresee enough benefit. You may gamble something because you see a potential reward. Plus, the risk of rejection is low since you can always blame bad luck.

When there is potentially damaging personal *failure*, for whatever reason (lack of preparation, unknown factors, lack of energy, etc.), some people will avoid or give up, allowing their Brain Stems to protect them (flight). Other people will become defensive or defiant (fight). Truly confident people will heed that failure warning. It triggers them to more consciously think through the situation to make a more thoughtful, rational decision as to whether they should attempt or avoid the situation. Confidence doesn't give them courage to take risks. Confidence also means you give yourself the right to avoid situations if and when you don't have enough information to decide whether the possible outcomes outweigh the potential failures.

Regret is also an unwanted result which deters some people from acting or even avoiding to decide. It is essentially also fearing potential failure but often is associated with the loss of something—materially, emotionally, egotistically. The risk of regret lights up the Amygdala which must then delegate the response either up into the analytical Prefrontal Cortex, or down into the brawny Brain Stem. Product and service warranties were designed to reduce the risk of regret to enable more confident purchase decisions. *Plan Bs* and other backup strategies help us avoid failure and any sense of regret.

Perhaps most threatening to our confidence is the *fear of rejection*. Without giving an entire Maslow lesson here (see *"Kickass Confidence"* or just look up Maslow's Hierarchy of Needs), back in 1940, Abraham Maslow transformed the way we understand human behavior.[32] To this day, it is the foundation of psychology and sociology. You can trace it into Cognitive Behavior Therapy (CBT), Neurolinguistic Programming (NP), and everything related to positive psyche. More relevant for us, it explains most every human action, reaction, and interaction.

Maslow's Hierarchy of Human Needs

As Maslow and thousands of his subsequent students promote, every human—of every age, race, gender, lifestyle, etc.—needs to feel a sense of ***belonging***. We may fulfill this through family and friends or from our work, religion, sports, associations, volunteerism, or other affiliations. We all need to know we are part of something. We need to know that we matter to the outside world.

The topic of belonging is making a big comeback in professional development books, through motivational presentations, and in diversity and inclusion (D&I) programs, because despite our modern hyper-connectiveness, we feel more isolated than ever. Belonging is technically an emotional *want*. Maslow labeled it a *need*, I do believe it is an emotional vitamin or critical ingredient that allows us to function well. Maslow said we can't reach our full potential without it. I say without (enough) belonging, we simply can't be confident.

If we sense that we may be rejected—disliked, outcast, or just uncool—the danger alarm is triggered and again, the Amygdala must choose where in the brain to send that. If it goes downstairs, the Brain Stem reacts by triggering behaviors such as shyness, mumbling, aggressiveness, defensiveness, disingenuousness, etc. If it takes the harder path upstairs, the Prefrontal Cortex can help us realize that we may be misjudging the situation, overreacting, or otherwise realize that we just shouldn't care that much.

The Amygdala essentially makes a choice that enables us to act with thoughtfulness and subsequent confidence—or it can mindlessly pick the path that causes us to act irrationally. It is a choice we can more consciously make when we better recognize the fear triggers. When we deliberately take the mental high road to our Prefrontal Cortex, we stay authentically aligned with our values (Prefrontal Cortex), wants (Limbic System), and needs (Brain Stem). We stay balanced on our life bicycle so we can drive ahead with confident thoughts, decisions, and behaviors.

Confidence Villains & Kryptonite

Everyone can use more confidence, though not everyone is confident enough to admit that. It is this denial that creates confidence-killing, villainous but all too common behavior. It happens so often that we are numb to this bullying that steals confidence from everyone.

Confidence may be weakened by many things that we usually can't control, such as trauma, injury, chemicals, or genetic causes. Even with a healthy brain and *normal* circumstances, our confidence is still poked at throughout our lives. Everyday living requires us to make constant decisions. Our confidence is tested every time we act, react, and interact.

As you should appreciate now, confidence is a winning asset. It is true power that real-life villains want to steal. Villains can be situations, other people, or even ourselves. Unfortunately, villains are all around us—so much so that we don't even see them. Villains want to diminish our confidence by creating fear of failure, regret, and rejection.

Confidence Stealing Situations

Whether it is the first time or not, some situations are exciting, others are terrifying. Theoretically, the more you do something, the more familiar and less scary it becomes. Yet, it does not always work that way. Sometimes the more you do something, the more you convince yourself it IS scary. Don't ask me to see a horror movie or to snowboard. Some situations just don't get easier or less confidence challenging. We learn that we aren't competent at something, which makes us fear doing it even more. One could argue that eventually you do overcome that fear, but the obvious counterargument is you first must be confident that you even *want* to overcome that fear.

Depending on the type of situation, some people may embrace the challenge, while others recoil. Consider how you feel about these types of situations:

- Interviewing for a job

- Making a big purchase like a house or car

- Presenting or pitching an idea/company/product

- Competing in something like a trivia game or intellectual contest

- Being personally assessed for any type of competency or other measurement

If you are saying, "bring them on," it's because you enjoy the adrenaline rush of novelty and/or winning. Maybe you are leaning on past similar successes. Maybe you are a thrill seeker who is simply wired for adventure. Maybe you confidently (or overconfidently) assume that you will figure out a way to accomplish those things.

If you are thinking, "please poke my eyes out instead," you're in the majority. Putting yourself into a new, potentially losing situation can be scary. There is good reason since these situations all commonly trigger the big three confidence fears of failure, regret, or rejection.

In confidence-challenging situations, our Amygdala lights up to warn us of pending emotional danger. We've been socially trained to think of those situations as personal tests because they judge our competence, intelligence, and most certainly, our belonging. Failure feels lousy. Our Amygdala wants to protect us from that. But instead of helping us strategically cope, it is easier to let the Brain Stem take over. We then hunker down hoping we can avoid the situation or just quickly get through it.

When we identify what the fear is, we can more consciously deal with it. Whenever we sense fear, we need to start seeing it as a sign or notification. It is our Amygdala's warning of potential emotional danger. You may feel nervous, agitated, angry, frustrated, or depressed. As a result, you may sweat, have an escalated heart rate, feel pain, or experience other autonomic responses. Recognizing these signs is the first step to managing the fear and rerouting the control to the Prefrontal Cortex. Instead of freaking out with Brain Stem caveperson-like behavior, we can remain calm and confident with our Prefrontal Cortex in command of our brain, body, and behaviors.

In addition to situations, sometimes other people steal our confidence simply because they need more of it themselves. In many cases, people rob confidence without even knowing they are doing it. This behavior is so common, we accept it and sometimes even reward it. My guess is that as you read further, you'll realize that you, too, have unconsciously stolen other people's confidence.

Bonehead Behaviors

While Confidence Imposters are more personality types that consistently try to steal confidence, there are times when even well-intentioned people slip into villain mode. Bonehead Behaviors happen because someone is mindlessly trying to survive by defending their ego. That person needs to feel a sense of belonging and to confirm that they matter. Perhaps ironically, the behaviors are easily recognizable as signs of insecurity—usually even to the actor. The Bonehead Behavior may work at that moment, but it doesn't sustain confidence and the person later often regrets acting that way. These behaviors are clearly a form of *fight* triggered by the Brain Stem.

Example Bonehead Behaviors are:

- **"Smartest Person in the Room."** This is the supposed expert or *know it all* who rudely corrects others in a public setting (e.g. "No, you are wrong. It is not 10.2, it is 10.24.").

The correction may be accurate but often is done in a way that unnecessarily embarrasses the erroneous person. It is done for the satisfaction of the corrector by proving he/she is superior.

Another form of *Smartest Person in the Room* is someone who uses big alienating words or acronyms, technical tidbits, or even other sources of expertise. They may say, "Have you read X?", or "Are you familiar with Y?" Those references may be intended to help until the person then adds, "I'm surprised that you don't know them/that." The *Smartest Person in the Room* wants to establish and maintain themselves as THE authority to feel important, unchallengeable, and controlling.

• **Talking Over**. This is when one person tries to speak with others but is simply not allowed to get a word in edgewise. The person being Talked Over may not even be *allowed* to answer questions directed to him/her. Being Talked Over makes the victim feel small and unvalued. Unfortunately, I hear this a lot from women who get talked over by BOTH men and other women.

• **Interrupting**. It's terribly frustrating when someone interrupts your thoughts and cuts you off mid-sentence. It is a derivative of being talked over, but sometimes other people aren't completely overriding your contributions; they are impatiently imposing their words and control of the conversation. The interrupter is not actively listening, which isn't just disrespectful, it demonstrates a lack of interest in the other person.

• **Distracted**. Popular forms of distracted behaviors include frequently checking a mobile device, looking past your face when talking to you, or being clearly preoccupied with something other than what you are discussing. It is disrespectful and challenges other people's confidence.

- **Gossiping**. Talking behind someone's back to another person(s) is wrong, but it happens all the time. We may even unintentionally encourage a form of gossiping through interpersonal assessments and awareness training. Unfortunately, while designed to help, if not well-managed these can create labels and expectations that diminish some people's confidence.

- **One Upping**. This is when someone tells you they have done or own something better than you just described. The opposite of this is also an Imposter: The **One Downing**. Someone whose ill fortune is worse than yours ("You had the flu for only three days? I had it for ten."). Both one upping and one downing are aimed to make you feel less impressive.

- **Any form of "I know a guy."** Other than someone who genuinely wants to help, name dropping can be a way to demote other people, too. People who flaunt their supposed network without being helpful connectors are bragging about their *belonging*. It never surprises me to find out that they often don't even know those connections well. They may know *of* them or superficially be *connected* online. Yet, they want everyone to think they have a powerful, enviable network of friends and fans.

Right now, you may be laughing because I bet you have experienced firsthand or even done these Bonehead Behaviors. The good news is we all have. The bad news is that whether conscious or not, they are attempts to steal other people's confidence. If we were explaining this to kids, we'd use a word for it: bullying.

All Too Common Bullying

Consider that the definition of a bully is someone who diminishes other people in some way to feel better about himself/herself. Bonehead Behaviors accomplish that. The bully tries to raise their own value by devaluing other people. Even when we recognize the bad behavior, we may self-doubt or worse, we may socially accept this and allow our confidence to be stolen.

As a result, victims feel embarrassed, demotivated, frustrated, and may even withdraw from all future interactions with that bully and the witnesses. The victims may shut down and not contribute their ideas, opinions, or perspectives so they avoid further alienation. Bullies are toxic—like fictional villains, they recruit followers and create cults. They kill creativity and innovation. They prevent engagement, collaboration, and trust. Like cancer in organizational culture, Bonehead Behaviors can kill confidence and all productive human contribution.

Criticism Can Crush Confidence

Confidence can certainly be compromised by criticism. Jealous, angry, and insecure people often use criticism as their weapon of choice to hurt other people. Depending on when and how the criticism is delivered, it can make a huge difference in how it is received and used. The relationship with and respect for the person giving the criticism also impacts how it may be received.

Criticism received from authorities, teachers, or leaders tends to have greater impact because we value their opinions and want their acceptance. Criticism is more powerful when it comes from anyone who we trust and want acceptance from, such as our friends and teammates. Even if you don't like or respect the person, he/she may deliver feedback that crushes your confidence. Whether solicited or not, criticism can unexpectedly jolt your Amygdala and trigger a caveperson, Brain Stem reaction such as getting defensive or depressed.

Parental criticism can be the hardest on confidence. Even if we recognize that our parents may be wrong or hypercritical, it is close to impossible to ignore negative feedback. As parents, we rarely realize the omnipotent impact we have on our kids. Everything we say and do is heeded in some subliminal way.

Any time, at any age, and in any way that a parent criticizes (or ignores), it can deeply hurt a child. Why? Because parents are our foundational fans and when we seemingly let them down, it taps into our sense of belonging, safety, and overall survival. Even if we are fully independent, parental criticism shakes up our Amygdala with a deafening alert that pushes us into Brain Stem-controlled caveperson mode. We want to matter to the people we care about, especially to our parents.

It helps to realize that even intentionally spiteful criticism, can be used productively. Consider criticism as data that you then decide to either use or discard. Use criticism to detect that person's intentions and then choose to store or ignore the feedback. Remember that one person's opinion is just that, even if you respect and want to please that person. *Choosing to let things roll off your back* without being indifferent is a hallmark of confident people. I realize that this is easier to write than it is to do.

Confidence Itself Can Be Intimidating

Confident people can also wig out less confident people.

That may seem like a strange comment given that truly confident people want to make other people feel confident. However, it takes both sides of that equation to work. The confident person must want to share their confidence with the other person AND the *not confident* person needs to want to welcome the available confidence. When there is an imbalance, confident people can actually be off-putting.

Self-Induced Confidence Killers

While we like to think of other people as villains, we may also be responsible for killing our own confidence. When faced with one of the confidence fears (failure, regret, rejection), we tell ourselves that we can't do something, we aren't worthy, or we're never lucky. We conclude that we are faking it, unqualified, perhaps lazy. Some of the resulting psychosocial conditions have gained names and subsequent notoriety:

- **Imposter Syndrome**. A feeling that you are faking or otherwise unqualified to do something like a job or task. *"I hope they don't find out I'm really not that good at this."*[33]

- **Application Avoidance**. Not applying or otherwise trying to do something because you feel you lack capability or potential, as demonstrated by the previously referenced 2014 Harvard Business Review study that claimed women needed to feel 100% qualified to apply for the same job that men only needed 60% confirmation.[34] This study has had recent resurrection in efforts to improve recruiting processes to enable gender equitable application pools.

- **Fear of Missing Out (FOMO)**. A feeling that you are not doing something at least as equally impressive as your friends on Facebook or other social channels. Whether an event, experience, or general lifestyle, the curated content of someone's social media can cause us to feel inferior and/or that we're missing out on things we *should* be doing. Even though we intuitively know the information may be very far from the truth, we often still feel like losers and left out. Researched deeply at my alma mater, University of Pennsylvania, FOMO has been provably linked to clinical depression.[35]

These are just some of the ways we trigger our own irrational, insecure thoughts, and subsequent Brain Stem-controlled bad behavior. As a result, we are less open to new ideas or actions. We hunker down to protect ourselves from more potential emotional harm. Or worse, we do Bonehead things to steal other people's confidence. The movie "Mean Girls" is funny because it is so real. Now you know neurologically why.

Confidence Kryptonite

These confidence villains have been around forever and will continue to exist. Unfortunately, confidence is even more challenged today by the confidence kryptonite of overchoice and decision fatigue mentioned in Part 1.

We don't necessarily have more choices today to make, we have more choices per choice. It takes so much mental energy to decide what to watch on TV, what salad dressing to buy, what apps to use, etc. For every choice we want or need to make, we can usually find an infinite number of options. Thanks to the internet, globalization, and other assumed productivity advances, our brains are so taxed with the number of options, that we are often unable to think straight. We run out of neural resources or require so many at any one time that our brains literally shut down. Like a computer, we then operate in a reduced capacity-like *safe mode*—or even have our system crash. And like a computer, the only way to reboot it is to turn our brains off by going to sleep.

Sleep Washing

Arianna Huffington, founder of Huffington Post and author of several books, is a crusader for sleeping more.[36] Her research shows that serious car accidents happen more often as a result of tired drivers than drunk ones. Tired brains can't make good decisions, let alone confident ones. While you shouldn't operate heavy equipment or sign contracts when you are under the influence of any drug, that's also worthy advice when you are just plain pooped. If you're too tired to control your brain, it is impossible to control your driving, your mouth, or any behavior.

Your brain needs sleep not just as fuel, but to clear your mental pollution. While you sleep, your brain prunes unnecessary neural paths that waste cognitive resources and potentially tangle up higher priority pathways. Research also says that sleep helps remove a type of brain plaque (amyloid beta) that may cause, or at least contribute to, Alzheimer's and other neurological decline. Sleep helps your brain stay clear so you can make confident decisions about everything. It just may save your career, relationships, and possibly your life.

Metaconfident Thinking

> *Metaconfident Thinking is proactively planning how you will manage emotional alerts before they result in impulsive, potentially regrettable, <u>not confident</u> results. By habitually pushing thinking up into our confidence-creating Prefrontal Cortex, we can stay calmer and more present. We can make better decisions about everything, including how we want to behave.*

Today's leadership buzzword is "authentic," but people rarely know what it really means. Search the "definition of authentic self" and you'll find a variety of answers about being genuine, but it doesn't give us a sense of how to *behave genuinely.*

ACI's stab is that being authentic means unapologetically being who you want to be, and not what is socially demanded or expected. You are not embarrassed by your strengths or weaknesses and you don't mask or change your personality to accommodate other people or situations. This transparency requires courage, self-compassion, resilience, and all the other Confidence Cousins. But as we noted before, the Cousins all lack the desired amount of information to confirm confidence. They are behavioral drivers in the *absence* of certainty.

Authentic Confidence Requires More Than Being Authentic

When we don't *know* the possible outcomes and *respond* instinctually, we may be authentic, but we may negatively impact others. Acting with unabashed authenticity sounds freeing, but if it creates interpersonal friction, it can prevent you from getting what you really value, need, and want. We can trigger other people's insecurities or be otherwise disrespectful. Their response may then be unexpected, difficult to deal with, and counterproductive. Therefore, authenticity in the absence of social awareness works *against* your confidence.

Figuring out your own strengths, weakness, priorities, and potential is undoubtedly key to self-confidence. Nonetheless, we cannot, nor should we, turn off our mirror neurons that allow us to learn from other people. Being authentic doesn't mean being 100% original, but rather a unique combination of other people's traits that you choose to adopt or reject. Therefore, *imitating* confidence is completely recommended if it is intentional. This doesn't make you inauthentic or a fake. It makes you growth-minded and in my book, brilliant.

Thoughts About Thoughts

Most personality and many behavioral assessments typically insist that you are who you are, and you can't change that wiring. I do not subscribe to that belief. When you take control of your thoughts, I believe and have seen hundreds of times that we can change our mindsets, behaviors, and personalities. Equally proven, we can change the way we respond to situations, other people's behaviors, and their personalities. We can also learn to stop self-sabotaging.

I have worked with clients all over the world and measured the change in their confidence. I know it is possible to proactively be the person you want to be—if you are willing to do the cognitive work.

It all starts with thinking about thinking. Psychologists call that a *metacognitive thought*: a thought about a thought. For example, you think about your thoughts any time you plan how you are going to do something, when you develop a test-taking strategy, or when you analyze why you feel some way about something.

This concept can also apply to confidence. At ACI, we coined the term *metaconfident thought* for when someone is consciously thinking about being confident. It is the conscious decision to be confident by taking control of your own brain. This means confidence doesn't miraculously happen, nor is it an entitled result. Metaconfident Thinking is a skill that is intentionally practiced and mastered.

Thinking Is Harder Than You Think

Unfortunately, *thinking* takes effort to do and even more effort to remember to do repeatedly. And like physical fitness, it is easier to be weak and lazy. Thinking can be hard work depending on the familiarity or confidence of an individual with a specific task. Consider that doing a crossword puzzle or math problem may be enjoyable for some but torturous for others.

Brain training is akin to physical conditioning. You deliberately exercise various regions of the brain to strengthen the associated neural pathways and patterns.

Fortunately, you don't need a Ph.D. to master Metaconfident Thinking. Enlightened yogis and spiritual leaders perform Metaconfident Thinking. Surely Gandhi, Mandela, and King were master metaconfident thinkers. Elite athletes, military, and C-Suite executives now use mindfulness and seek peak performance through Metaconfident Thinking with the help of emotional coaches. Their aim is to eliminate emotional noise, allowing the coachee to maintain focus and quickly get into the zone/flow. In this state of heightened consciousness, the mind and body are so connected that there is unwavering focus, control, and confidence. People describe being in *the zone* as having a "Matrix Moment,"[37] where time slows down, enabling you to "avoid targeted bullets or other confidence challenges." You can effortlessly focus on an important task without distraction. Basketball Hall of Famer Larry Bird was one of the first to describe the mind-body connection on the court with his consistent success on the free throw line.

We all go in and out of flow while typing at our computers, driving our cars, cooking, or doing something that requires our focus. If you have ever looked up and gasped at how much time has flown by, it's because when you're in *the zone*, you feel so calm and in control of everything—your mind, body, and time. Coming out of flow is literally a rude awakening, realizing the rest of the world kept moving at its normal pace. Athletes, sharpshooters, and other high-performance professionals proactively train their brains to get into flow faster. You can, too.

Burpees for Your Brain

Brain training apps such as Lumosity, Fit Brains, and Elevate are built on the *memory muscle* theory—if you exercise the specific parts of your brain such as the ones that enable memory, you can strengthen those parts. In addition to such research evidence, I have asked thousands of people in my presentations about their experiences using such apps. Every person tells me they like the apps and that the apps help them improve memory and focus. Nevertheless, the same people say they didn't continue using the apps because the apps lack *stickiness*. Users get bored or assume they will just remain mentally fit without further effort. Unfortunately, this is not true. "Use it or lose it" applies to your neural pathways, too. Mind muscles are just like muscles in your arms. They atrophy when not used, and in the case of your brain, you may even lose the new pathways when the brain does its normal neural pruning. Therefore, to sustain the desired ability, you must continue to use the associated neural pathways and exercise your brain, just as you would continually condition your body.

It is not surprising to read that any type of behavior or habit change is hard. Entire books and studies are focused on the neuroscience of habit change, which is outside the scope of this book. Still, as we discuss building sustainable confidence, we must consider that we are building new behavioral habits and therefore, our process here is (literally) mindful of our inevitable mental inertia. Any time you feel mentally challenged, it's because you are using, and perhaps pioneering, new neural pathways.

Some Eastern philosophies also strive to strengthen these mind/body connections, but believe they are enabled by an outside or spiritual higher power entity such as Qi, Ki, or Chakra. These philosophies follow the same notion that your brain isn't the ultimate decider of your thoughts—there is a higher power. Part of these beliefs include using the *subjective data* created by your subconscious, which is often unseen or ignored. As such, the Eastern philosophies emphasize the importance of having total brain control, not just the educated, intellectual parts of it.

In most religions, the idea of a higher power implies that our judgement and actions are guided by something bigger than our unaware brains. Religion involves much more than that concept, but at the core, higher power is a way to explain why and how we need to look beyond our own conscious thinking to fully understand and control ourselves.

Conditioning Confidence

If you are not spiritual, then at least consider that counting sheep is a common method to redirect the brain. Visual techniques such as using a focal point, mind map, or counting something all require Prefrontal focus and therefore, a calmer brain. Communication methods such as journaling are scientifically proven to work, too, as they cause the Prefrontal Cortex to process thoughts and rationalize behaviors.[38] Most psychological and coaching modalities use communication as a diagnostic and curative method—especially Cognitive Behavioral Therapy (CBT) which is fundamentally based on self-awareness and communication.

Thoughts don't easily just melt or fly out of our brains. Even when pushed into the back of your head or other places that aren't as seemingly active, negative thoughts can remain in your subconscious brain and manifest in other ways through your behaviors and body. Many mind/body medical professionals profess the impact of repressed thoughts that can create or exaggerate bodily malfunctions—everything from back/neck/shoulder/hip/ knee/elbow/wrist/etc. pain, to incontinence, and neurological conditions such as radial neuropathies, Parkinson's, Multiple Sclerosis (MS), and some Dystonias.[39]

The worrisome Amygdala alarms continue to fire and are grabbed fast by the Brain Stem instead of the more thoughtful Prefrontal Cortex. Eventually the Amygdala finds an alarm ally in some body part that starts hurting and sending pain as warning signs of the suppressed stress.

Further hard evidence of mind/body medical miracles is the fascinating research being done around placebos.[40] The data proves that in many situations, we can cure ourselves without medicine simply by *thinking* ourselves better. Strangely, there is data to suggest that even when we *know* it is a placebo, we can still invoke our brain to address the condition.

I've seen people willfully change their pulse, body temperature, and other autonomic functions. I've seen my own son control the genetically-caused dystonia that causes a disconnect between his brain and arms. I've even used mindfulness to cure my own elbow tendinitis and persistent leg cramping. People in my confidence workshops constantly report similar successes. And while it may not be the cure-all for everyone or every issue, trying a mind/body method can be an easy, non-invasive solution without causing harmful side-effects. With little to no cost, trying to mend your body with your mind is at least worth a try—provided you have your doctor's clearance.

The only caveat to attempting mind-body solutions is that you must have confidence that it *could* work with a commitment to try beyond a single attempt. Time and patience are required. You can't just flip a mental switch to build or repair a neural pathway no more than you can mentally heal a broken bone.

Neuroplasticity is one of the most exciting concepts in neuroscience. It is the ability to physically change the neural pathways that control your thoughts, behaviors, and even body. A subset of neuroplasticity is neurogenesis which means you can also create *new* neural pathways. Scientists have proved beyond any shadow of doubt, that even into our 70's, our brains continue to morph as long as their owners try.[41] The brain remains plastic and open to new ideas, information, and challenges such that you can learn anything that you put your mind to. There may be physical reasons that limit neuroplastic change, such as brain damage, genetic or environmentally caused mutations, trauma, stress, drugs/ medications, malnutrition, exhaustion, etc.

With enough health and a positive attitude, neuroplasticity is already enabling many patients to train their brains to build/rebuild neural highways that help them to better physically drive their bodies. Using neuroplastic techniques such as movement therapy, there are doctors, clinics, and independent practitioners working with patients to repair or reroute damaged neural pathways. This is already a typical part of most stroke treatment plans. Other neurological diseases are following these techniques so that patients can rebuild the broken neural pathways that cause a disconnect between their brain and body.

There is great hope to remedy neurological conditions, by reconnecting or rerouting the neural chain. Once retrained, the movement message gets repeated until it solidly fuses so the patient can effectively trigger the movement with just their own *normal* brain-to-body thoughts.

For more on physical manifestations and using mind/body therapies, look into the various works of Dr. Rob Sarno, Dr. Joaquin Faris, or Dr. Norman Dodge.

Prescription medications are widely used to calm a busy mind or pep up a lazy one. Meditation and other forms of mindfulness are also very popular ways to induce brain focus and readiness. Whether using an app, recording, mantra, or any other method to induce calm, the intent is to get the brain to pay attention to the neural training.

Non-invasive processes are usually repeated over time to achieve sustainable results. Different methods, intensities, and durations work for different people. There are many ways to stimulate the brain and create neuroplasticity.

As Frankensteinian as it sounds, even today electricity and magnetism are used often to stimulate the brain—essentially get it to pay attention—so it is receptive to the retraining. One such highly successful method is Deep Brain Stimulation (DBS) which surgically implants what is essentially a pacemaker in the brain. It is now a relatively common treatment option for otherwise unresponsive cases of Tourette Syndrome, Parkinson's, and Dystonia. Electric Shock Therapy (more modernly called Electroconvulsive Therapy (ECT)) is still used along with similar but less invasive methods such as Magnetic Seizure Therapy (MTS) and Transcranial Magnetic Stimulation (TMS). Some patients even find over time that they no longer need the artificial stimulation to maintain control of those body parts. In some cases, the original neuropathy is corrected but another one develops somewhere else in the body (perhaps because the actual cause of the problem hasn't been addressed). These treatments and results are still nascent for us to better understand longer-term neuroplastic possibilities. I truly believe it will soon be pervasive practice to scientifically train our brains to heal our bodies.

The various medical and non-traditional approaches have pros and cons, risks, and potential side effects. *Therefore, please protect us both and be sure to consult your doctor if you are going to try any type of treatment.* Just don't be discouraged if your doctor doubts the power of less invasive solutions. At least one of you needs to be confident that there *could* be positive results.

Making Confidence Your Default Choice

Let's get back to our own focus on confidence and Metaconfident Thinking. Using the brain science that explained a bit how thinking works and how it best learns, ACI uses the following process to build strong, repeatable confidence pathways. Our goal is to give you the knowledge and tools to be confident, especially when your confidence is challenged.

Here is ACI's process for Metaconfident Conditioning:

CLARIFY: Be clear about what confidence is and what it is not; know how confidence works in the brain and how it impacts behavior; recognize things that challenge confidence and realize that you can control your brain and behavior. (All Done!)

CALIBRATE: Measure and monitor confidence. Identify what is driving versus diminishing it. (All done!)

CONTROL: Get tools to manage confidence and make confident decisions, especially when dealing with difficult people or situations. Have techniques to realign confidence when it is kicked off course.

COMMUNICATE: Convey confidence through all forms of verbal and non-verbal communication.

COACH: Even informally, help others gain confidence in themselves. This isn't just benevolent. When others are confident, you also gain confidence and it makes it easier for you to influence them, too.

Let's keep going.

# Part 3: CONTROL

Master Your Mindset

> *Mindset is the foundation for what we think and subsequently, what we do. Therefore, having the 'right' mindset allows us to build and maintain strong confidence.*

Dictionary.com defines mindset as:

Mindset is the ideas and attitudes with which a person approaches a situation, especially when these are seen as being difficult to alter.

Mindsets filter what we think. Mindset forms from information that we are taught or gain from experiences. Our mindsets can be assets or liabilities since they drive our thoughts and habits/behaviors—whether these may or may not be desired.

To rid yourself of an undesired thought or behavior, it usually helps to replace it with a desired one. For example, you might start chewing gum because you want to stop biting your nails. You want to sleep better so you start using a meditation app instead of playing a mobile game before going to bed. Some habits are, of course, harder to replace than others. All behavior change requires us to redirect the habitual neural *routes* in our brains that trigger subsequent behaviors.

With new information and a willingness to consider this information, you can change your mindset. I previously referenced Carol Dweck's now famous work on the Growth Mindset[42] which implies that people who want to learn are more successful. Growth minded people don't stay stuck on an ignorant or disserving mindset. They seek out new and potentially improved perspectives. They identify more productive thinking that creates desired thoughts, habits, and overall behaviors.

Perhaps you started reading this book with a mindset that confidence is not something you can control or choose. After reading the first few chapters, I hope your mindset shifted!

As we discussed previously, you decide (consciously or unconsciously) if and how you will approach every situation. Your mindset is an overlay or lens that then impacts your motivation and attitude. For example, I decide that I should take a run outside (attitude), but I'm not excited to do it (motivation). While I believe I could and should do it (confidence), I find all kinds of excuses to avoid doing it because in the past, I remember that running was uncomfortable and time consuming (mindset). I end up not running because my mindset won't overcome the challenges, even if I am confident about my ability to do it. Therefore, having an aligned mindset is critical to making and executing confident decisions.

Mindset Impacts Everything

The adage says "attitude is everything"—well, sort of. Attitude is more situational and transient. Your attitude can change depending on an infinite number of variables and is often the manifestation (behaviors, habits, communication, etc.) of your mindset, general thoughts, motivations, and intentions. Mindset is more fixed.

As an example, I realized a while back that watching or reading the news in the morning caused me to have a negative attitude all day. Hearing about violence and other social problems put a black cloud over my head all day. However, my mindset was that I didn't want to be like that and needed a way to change it. I therefore asked my husband to notify me if any major news happened so I wouldn't be in danger or have total social ignorance. Now, I read weekly publications so I can catch up on past news that has since lost its potency.

Regardless of the subtle differences, just remember you can change both your attitude and your mindset.

The following techniques are proven true ways to master your own mindset so you can set and reset it as needed. They are very easy and enable Metaconfident Thinking so you can consciously activate your Prefrontal Cortex. It is also theorized by some notable scientists that these exercises pump your brain with motivating neurotransmitters (e.g. dopamine, adrenaline, oxytocin, etc.) while reducing negative, unproductive ones (e.g. cortisol).[43]

Try one or more of these techniques to see which works for you and use it every time you feel your mindset turns south into Brain Stem territory—that is, when you aren't feeling confident. Like any new behavior, shifting your mindset takes some time and mental energy, but the process, as well as the result, makes a monumentally positive difference in your confidence.

Talking to Yourself Isn't Crazy—Just the Opposite

Self-talk is a popular method to help manage mindset. It seems easy in concept, but you need a way to ensure that any existing self-defeating attitude and mindset doesn't make you feel worse.

Here are some prompts to help change negative self-talk into more positive, productive thoughts:

- How can I change the current/resulting situation?

- What's the worst that can happen next?

- What can I learn from this experience?

- How can I avoid this in the future?

- What would I tell someone else who is experiencing the same situation?

These questions help find the silver lining in situations by acknowledging the problem, keeping it in perspective, and then using the experience to grow forward. As you use these mindset prompts, remember that you are still human and thus, you are absolutely expected to err at least occasionally. Often, you just don't have an accurate perception of a situation. You'll naturally see it much worse than others, perhaps even irrationally. An objective thought partner is great when you can access one but if not, use these prompts to coach yourself.

Your Brain Will Thank You

The hottest self-help trend these days is gratitude. We are told in books, articles, calendars, posters, blogs, and elsewhere to be thankful. This practice has been proven to override negative neural pathways and regain perspective. Some people start and/or end each day with a gratitude moment. Some people keep a gratitude journal or have another process for capturing gracious thoughts. Start catching yourself when you are feeling sad or angry and try to think of something in your life for which you are grateful.

You can be thankful for what you have, who you are, what you've accomplished, what you are experiencing—essentially anything. That's the good and bad news. There are a ton of choices, but it is unclear what the best types and optimal ways are to practice gratitude. It doesn't hurt to give gratitude a go and see if this very simple and free mindset shift helps remind you, even if things aren't ideal and are out of your control at that moment. Many people find benefit from writing down or sharing over dinner three things they are grateful for every day. One of them could even be having control of your confidence.

Make Someone's Day Every Day

A truly easy habit to start is to go out of your way every day to give someone else an authentic compliment. Give them an immediate serotonin boost by letting them know they *belong* by complimenting how they look, something they did, or just that you appreciate your relationship with them. You can convey the compliment in writing, such as a text or email, but nothing has the same impact as friendly eye contact and a welcoming smile. Warm up an interview, set a confident tone in a meeting, or just build rapport when you need help from someone by simply saying, "I like your {fill in the blank}."

Another neurotransmitter known as the *cuddle drug* is oxytocin, which can be triggered from human touch. While laws, policies, and social mores prevent us from freely touching everyone, when appropriate, consider a handshake, a pat on the shoulder, or give someone a hug (be sure to ask first if they are cool with that). All these physical gestures can amp up all the other ways you let someone know they matter. Again, just be very smart about when, how, and who you touch. Touches can have magical confidence powers, but used wrongly, they can be socially and politically risky.

Blow Down a Negative Mindset with Three Little Things

Breathing, like self-talk and gratitude, allows you to activate your Prefrontal Cortex, to have control of the rational part of your brain and subordinate the potentially wild Brain Stem. However, some people or situations get the best of you and just put you in a bad mood. It may be easiest to ride out the negative storm of emotions by acknowledging "this too shall pass." One technique we use at the Institute that helps shortcut recovery is called *Three Little Things*.

Rather than a list of random things for which you are thankful, identify three things that consistently make you happy. They must be things that you can easily buy, do, or otherwise get on-demand. They can be anything such as a favorite food, TV show, or an activity that you enjoy. Maybe you enjoy spending time on a hobby, in a specific place, or with a special person.

The key is to make the happy things concrete and something you can do relatively easily and immediately at any time. You shouldn't depend too much on other people or circumstances to do or have one of your Three Little Things.

For me, I love 1) Wegman's Marathon Bread; 2) playing board/card games; and 3) playing guitar with my husband and kids. When I eat/do any of these things, I am mindful of the pleasure they bring me. My Three Little Things allow me to realign my mindset and bring me back to a place of positivity and confidence. I am also reminded that I will get past the situation just as I did the last time I needed that happy thing.

What are your *Three Little Things*?

1)

2)

3)

Structures Are Mindset Spark Plugs

My favorite mindset method is something called a *Structure*. A Structure can be anything such as a motivational song, a memorable picture, a specific warm up routine, a comforting piece of clothing, or a long-time lucky charm. A Structure wakes up your brain by making you focus on something that is memorably positive. When you consciously look at, or even just envision it, the Structure sends your brain a message that you are capable. Your *Three Little Things* are essentially interactive Structures. Structures can also be intangible things that you look at, listen to, or otherwise just think about.

Athletes often use photos from prior wins. These photo Structures remind the athlete that they have won before and can again. The mental stimulus theoretically drips some of the neurotransmitter dopamine into their brains which makes the athlete feel competent, accomplished, and proud. It also fires up some adrenaline giving them the energy and excitement to perform.

Productively using nervous energy is a desired state called *Peak Anxiety*.[44] It is an essential part of high-performance training so the individual can use stress in a positive way to energize, not unnerve themselves. Watch Michael Phelps before he approaches a pool to race. He has earbuds playing songs that pump him up and a series of physical arm movements that warm up his body and his brain. Most baseball players have some pre-batting routine involving swinging the bat, tapping it with their cleats, and other warm-up motions they repeat every time at bat. While they may look bizarre, these specific movements are done so the athletes prime their brains. The warmup routine is a Structure that preps their Prefrontal Cortex, so they literally have their *head in the game* and their confidence ready to play.

Even if you are an amateur athlete, you're probably familiar with *Ready Position*, which is a way to position your body to prepare for the race or play.[45]

To get into a standing Ready Position, create a slight bend in your knees. Keep your feet hip-width apart and either parallel, or with one foot slightly in front of the other. The position of your feet will depend on the sport and/or your preference. Check to make sure your body weight is supported in the balls of your feet, so you're slightly leaning forward, ready to move ahead. Ready Position is, in fact, a Structure. It is a way to tell your body and brain, "Get ready – let's do this!"

In and out of sporting situations, you can use the same technique anytime your mindset needs a shot of confidence.

Stand Like Superwoman

Amy Cuddy's "Power Poses" are another great example of the mental power of physical Structures. Her Harvard-based research was recently reinstated as repeatable scientific results.[46] Watch her legendary TED Talk to hear Amy's premise that standing or sitting tall, like Wonder Woman or Superman, can create confidence in mere mortals. She suggests that the postures trigger positive neuro and hormonal transmission of dopamine and adrenaline, while also suppressing the stress-causing transmission of cortisol. She recommends *striking a pose* anytime you need a natural neuro-cocktail to give you confidence in a potentially stressful situation such as going into an interview or giving a presentation. Whether this helps because it is a ready position Structure or is a placebo effect, if it works for you, I say use it.

Find a Structure in your life that makes you recall a time you were confident. If possible, keep it physically handy or immediately doable. Start now by thinking about just one structure if you need an emergency shot of confidence.

Your Structure is:

____

Create a Confidence Collection

If you really want structure superpower, create a Confidence Collection. I have a Collection that I use every time I'm about to deliver a keynote. I swear to you that it immediately aligns my mindset and activates the engaging energy for which I am known.

To make one, just set up an online folder that you can easily access anytime. Fill the folder with emails, recommendations, and anything from other people that reflects something positive you did. Add photos, songs, videos, quotes—anything that brings you a smile. Before you are about to tackle an unpleasant or challenging task, peek through your Confidence Collection. It is mindset magic.

If you need it, a Confidence Collection can also help you recover afterwards when something doesn't go well. Use the Collection as confidence consolation to remember that despite that one not-so-great moment, you are still awesome.

Small but Mighty Mindset Movements

Another powerful mindset technique also borrowed by professional athletes is *small wins*. Rather than tackle a large goal such as shaving minutes off a race, athletes will set smaller goals such as a few seconds per week, or perhaps microseconds every few days. The small wins drip some powerful neurotransmitters that make them feel positive and motivated to repeat the winning experience. Consider habitual runners who often report being literally addicted to the adrenaline high.

Athletes also separate outcomes (win, lose, achieve) from their performance (how well they played) and the process (specific goals). This helps them keep a longer-range perspective and not give up after one poor play or game. They recognize improvement happens over time and inevitably includes bad spots or streaks. Study any pro tennis player and you will find that they overcame a time when they were losing a lot. Baseball players know they'll strike out more than they'll score. And every other sport is filled with stories of underdogs who eventually won just enough. Using small win goals, you too can continually reflect and celebrate even small successes that help you stay motivated toward desired outcomes.

Most behavior change programs use small wins, too. Consider Weight Watchers, which uses 2 lbs. per week or the Alcoholics Anonymous mantra of one day at a time. These are small win strategies to keep people motivated since habit change requires time and patience. Small wins help keep perspective and celebrate progress.

Accountabilibuddies*

Even the best athletes use coaches. The primary role of the coach is to have 3rd party eyes watching the athlete's performance, but also to help keep the athlete accountable toward ongoing performance goals.

A business, life, or other professional coach can do the same for you. A qualified coach will assist in creating a plan, objectively critiquing your performance, and helping you stay motivated with a positive mindset. He or she may use a variety of methodologies/modalities. They may require different ways to check in, celebrate progress, and regroup after failure. Professional coaches use a repeatable and measurable process. Both coach and coachee need to be honest, have faith, and trust one another.

While anyone can call themselves a coach and only a handful of credentialed certification programs exist, look for someone who is at least trained and/or highly experienced. A coach should be completely non-judgemental and be a thought partner. *(We'll discuss how YOU can be an everyday Confidence Coach for other people in our final chapter.)*

Mentors, friends, teachers, siblings—anyone can provide accountability coaching, or you may prefer using apps or other online tools. However, having to confess to another human being is perhaps the greatest motivator of all (fear of rejection).

*(*Thank you, David Israel, for introducing me to this clever portmanteau, which combined 2 words to coin a new one! Accountability + Buddy = accountabilibuddy.)*

Practice What We Preach

All the techniques presented are easy to do and if you do them often enough, they become autonomic responses. Use one or more whenever you need some mindset mojo to power through or recover from a confidence-challenging situation.

Putting this to practice, let's take a second to celebrate right now! Both of us are more than halfway done with the big task of a book— me writing it and you reading it. Let's mindfully celebrate that we are awesome.

Identify Your Values & Value

> *Knowing who you are and who you want to be may sound trivial or silly. You may be wondering why a neuro-based book would get so crunchy. The reason is quite simple: our values create necessary behavior filters for our brains so they can confidently choose how we should act, react, and interact.*

Asking what you *value* is a loaded question. Most people will answer with tangible, socially expected things, including having a loving family and friends, pets, hobbies, past experiences, and specific possessions. You are also likely to value intangible things such as how someone treats you or having constitutional rights. You may value your childhood or the charities you support. Anything you feel that is important or worth your time, attention, money, or effort is probably something you would note of value.

If I asked what your *values* are, you might instead select traits such as being compassionate, open-minded, generous, loving, honest, etc. I bet you also value having fun, a sense of humor, and good health.

According to the Oxford Dictionary:

"Values are principles or standards of behavior; one's judgement of what is important in life."

Words of Worth

The word *value* implies actual or perceived worth. Semantically, the word *values* is more absolute. You value a painting; being open-minded is one of your values.

Both value and values change over time depending on both external and internal factors reflecting what is needed or wanted at that moment. Most of us value napping much more now than we did when we were toddlers.

Value varies between people and can be greatly influenced by what other people perceive. If you are a collector, you know that not everyone sees the same value of whatever you collect. Some people aren't interested at all, while others will pay even more than you.

Your *values*, while influenced by other people, generally do not shift greatly as a result of other people's values, unless you consciously decide to change. Maybe you now value being organized since you want to respect your spouse's values. Or maybe in the past you were betrayed by a friend, so that loyalty is something you now value greatly.

To complicate things even further, *self-worth* is how much you value yourself and is often a reflection of how much you perceive that you are valued by other people. Yeesh! It is all quite confusing.

ACI asked more than 200 people over the age of 60 why their confidence finally peaked at 60. Their answers were consistent. They said they valued who they were and didn't care what other people thought. Sadly, it takes almost our entire life to achieve self-worth that isn't calibrated by guessing what we think other people are thinking.

Oftentimes I hear people complain that they don't feel valued, especially at work. They sense this because they aren't given *enough* responsibility, compensation, or overall respect in the workplace. Yet, when we pull apart that situation, it is often that they aren't respecting their own *values*. They may be making appropriate contributions to their organizations, but the work and/or environment itself isn't aligned with their own values. They assume there is something wrong **with** them in lieu of considering there is something wrong **for** them.

Notice the difference in these statements:

- "I need to leave my current job since I'm not being given career advancement opportunities."

vs.

- "I've decided to change jobs since my current one doesn't provide the professional development support that I want."

The first statement blames other people and circumstances. It does not take responsibility and implies unfairness. The second statement takes ownership and is proactive to satisfy one's own values without ill will. The former implies entitlement. The latter demonstrates confidence.

Confident people maintain values-based criteria in their brains that helps ensure they behave according to how they want to be known. They decide how to act/react based on their values, which are the rules and guidelines for their desired personal brand. The certainty of what they value dictates how they choose to behave.

They are also clear about the value they provide to other people and organizations; they appreciate how and why they are liked and needed. They don't minimize their contribution or worth, and when their *value* is questioned by their employer, a truly confident person will acknowledge the misalignment and choose to fix the situation or find a better match.

I have many personal examples where my values were challenged. I have worked for misogynistic managers. I have been part of management teams that manipulated accounting and/or people. I have been on both sides of an unexplainable layoff as well as unfair hiring. Each time, my values screamed in pain. Some of the times I tried to fix the situations for the good of the employees, myself, and my family. Other times I walked away to save my soul. When your values are being violated, it is the ultimate stressor that taxes your brain, body, and behaviors. Even now as ACI's CEO, I know if my values aren't aligned with my clients', I can't do my best work. I recognize too, that no one else can either.

You probably have your own similar example of accepting a job or negotiating for something and feeling like you were being undervalued or exploited. Most buyers negotiate with the objective to win the best possible deal. When you violate someone's values in that process, they will feel undervalued. When you bargain someone down, especially for some type of service engagement, you may win the deal monetarily, but overall lose value. They will never go above and beyond for you to deliver their best quality work. *Their* values won't allow it.

When YOU are the one being undervalued, don't look at the problem as anyone's fault. Objectively realize that the other person's perceived value is not aligned with your value, or values. For example, they may not be as responsive as you are. Maybe they don't get excited about doing something that you enjoy. Any time others disappoint you, it is because you have different values/priorities. This doesn't necessarily make either side wrong or bad. It just helps to know that they likely aren't choosing to offend you, but rather, they are choosing to honor their own values.

Hopefully it is obvious now that identifying your values is key to being your most confident, authentic, respected, and rewarded self. It isn't that easy and requires lots of experience, which is why it takes humans on average 60 years to figure it all out and reach our confident best.

There are few classes or tools to help and the ones out there are often contrived or complicated.

Here are two remarkably simple but highly effective exercises we use at ACI that can help you clarify your values:

Write Your "Youlogy"

As morbid and depressing as it may seem, this exercise is life empowering. It is the most impactful way, we have found at ACI, to help people identify their own values. Since your values are already swirling around in your head, you just need to filter them into your cognitive awareness without leading or making the process scripted, like circling words that you know are socially virtuous.

The *Youlogy* method is as follows:

Imagine that you just died and identify who you would like to give your eulogy. Next, write or type the eulogy, but don't put what you think *that person would say. Instead, write down what you would* want *him/her to say.*

Write as much as you like—there is no rule on how much. Just be honest with yourself about what you want to be *known for* and don't hold back on complimenting yourself. I highly recommend a glass of your favorite drink to relax and let your raw thoughts flow through your fingers. Don't analyze or obsess about the grammar or word choice. Just write. This isn't intended to be published. It's just a stream of semi-unconscious words to help bring forward your values into your conscious awareness. When you have your *Youlogy* written, circle words or phrases that describe you (e.g. a great listener, a loyal friend, a dedicated mother, etc.). Your chosen descriptors reflect your most prized values.

You may start to cry. You may feel frustrated or depressed about how your past doesn't quite reflect your desired legacy. All these feelings are common side effects and totally normal. The great news is that you have the rest of your life to become the person you really want to be—a person who exudes the values that YOU value. When we have those values-defined boundaries clear in our heads, we can act with less fear and more confidence.

At the end of every year (or more often as you like), pull out your *Youlogy* and see how you are doing. It is a moral compass like none other. You might want to update some of it, which is perfectly normal as you enter new life stages and gain more life experience. Many people use their *Youlogy* to set New Year's resolutions. The *Youlogy* reminds your brain of what is important so you can act, react, and interact with confidence.

Self-360

For decades, human resource professionals have used 360 Assessments to help individuals gain self-awareness through the eyes of their peers and colleagues. Essentially, 360s are done by asking other people for their positive and critical feedback about an individual. This method is known to have both pros and cons—giving someone external perspective at the risk of mixing in political motivations. 360 Assessments can hit people hard with the realities of what other people think about them. 360s may also make people think about a colleague more critically (potentially unnecessarily) than they normally would in day-to-day interactions. These and other reasons are why you don't hear as much about 360s anymore.

Taking the best of the concept, it can be extremely helpful to do your own 360 (aka a *Self-360*). Ask a few trusted people (two to three at least) to list five words that describe the type of person you are. Keep in mind, the feedback is relative to what you demonstrate to those people in your work role or associated persona. This may be very different than your *other* self, and how you behave when no one is looking. The exercise allows you to know what other people are seeing.

You can make this request in person or via electronic communication but either way, be sure to explain why you are asking them for this favor. For example, you can say:

"I'm doing a self-assessment exercise and would appreciate if you would email me back 5 words that you feel best describe me."

You aren't hunting for strengths, weaknesses, or advice. You just want their own one-word descriptors to confirm or add to the words in your *Youlogy*.

If any of the friends' words surprise you, go back to the person and ask with curious innocence why they chose that word. *DO NOT ARGUE, DEFEND, OR MANIPULATE THE FEEDBACK*. Listen to why they chose that word and thank them for the insight.

For extra valuable credit, after you have your friend's list, share your own list with them. Ask if he/she agrees with your selected words. This helps you identify the gaps where you can work towards better alignment between your values and behaviors. *Just don't share your own list until after you get their list.* This activity works only if you don't plant ideas into their head. Tell your friends to be totally honest with you. It is impossible to find friends who are unbiased, but you could add some people who aren't necessarily friends but more colleagues to your mix. You want their unaided and independently insightful words first. Only then will you be able to get their truthful confirmation about your words.

It may seem counterintuitive that to build confidence, I am suggesting that you care what other people think about you. This is seemingly opposite to ACI's confidence definition! Remember, other people's opinions are only just that, so we are only using their eyes to gain a clearer reflection of your own behavior, which you can't see in a regular mirror.

Stretch Before and After You Do These Exercises

Beware that your findings may cause you to be pleasantly satisfied and/or unexpectedly disappointed. Remember this is subjective *data* that you CHOOSE whether or not—and how—you want to use. Any type of exercises can be uncomfortable at times, including those that condition your confidence.

Needs & Wants

We all have basic survival and safety, Maslow-defined needs including eating, sleeping, sweating, sheltering, exercising, etc. We also discussed our pervasive *need* (which I argue is really a disguised want) to belong. Maslow also said we need to have self-esteem and actualization,[47] but it's a cagey argument that someone could die from a lack of confidence. Everything above Maslow's safety line is technically more want than need, unless you consider the mental health implications that might lead to severe physical consequences. A lack of belonging, self-esteem, or actualization (confidence) can certainly be linked to depression or worse. Whatever way that you categorize those hierarchy achievements, I believe we *need* them for our well-being.

In addition, there are other needs that are enablers, such as the need to earn income, be healthy, and get out into the sunshine. Let's agree that beyond basic physiological requirements, a need is also "something necessary to fulfill your values." Using my own example, I *need* a meaningful job. I *need* to spend quality time with my family. I *need* to sleep at least 7 hours a night. Without those things, I risk hurting myself physically, mentally, and emotionally.

These *needs* really are *wants*, but that would make them seem optional. When these needs aren't fulfilled, I can't be my confident best. I *want* to be confident and to do that, I *need* those elements, *e.g. I don't want to drive recklessly so I need to have enough sleep.* You could also say that you need to drive safely so you want to sleep enough.

Once again, the English language confuses the categories, in this case, the true meaning and difference of need vs. want. Whichever you use, it is important to be clear why you need or want something. This clarity of *why* is critical data that enables you to make confident decisions. Plus, perhaps obviously stated, when someone has unfulfilled wants or needs, it weakens their confidence. In this instance, *unfulfilled* means the person recognizes they want or need something, but then doesn't do anything (or do enough) to fulfill that want or need. The lack of action can cause shame, embarrassment, negativity, and other confidence-crushing side effects.

The Eight Key Confidence Indicators (KCIs)

In *"Kickass Confidence,"* I described the pervasive eight life buckets called Key Confidence Indicators (KCIs). ACI's research showed that these commonly recognized life needs directly impact everyone's core confidence. KCIs provide you a quick way to check on your general living needs that support a confident life.

When any KCI level isn't full *enough*, it can trigger one or all three of the fears—failure, regret, rejection—that negatively impact confidence. Like gauges in your car that indicate if there is enough oil, gas, air, and other necessary elements to drive your car confidently, KCIs can do the same for your everyday life. They help you to monitor your confidence vital signs for optimal operation of the vehicle—in this case, you!

The *Eight KCIs* are as follows:

1.   Mental & Physical Health

2.   Education & Street Smarts

3.   Financial & Career Security

4.   Pastimes & Possessions

5.   Beauty & Personal Care

6.   Sleep & Think Time

7.   Faith & Protection

8.   Human Support & Connections

Personal Confidence Dashboard & Plan

The KCIs can be used to create a Personal Confidence Dashboard to visually identify whether any of your KCIs need more attention at that given time. The process is simple. Rank yourself on a scale of 1 (lowest) to 5 (highest) based on how well you manage each Key Confidence Indicator (KCI).

If you want to use a more quantitative approach, you can use the questions below.

Do one KCI at a time and for each question to which you answer Yes, give yourself one point for that KCI. Color in your point totals below to get a visual observation of your current overall core confidence.

1.   Can you justify the time and money you spend (or don't spend) on this?

2.   Do you feel in control of this KCI more than 75% of the time?

3.   Do you take deliberate action to improve this KCI every week?

4. Do you have realistic benchmarks to accurately measure your level in this KCI?

5. Do you have a response mechanism to take action when this KCI is stressed?

A sample Personal Confidence Dashboard is shown below. The height of the bars reflects the person's confidence in each of the KCIs. In this example, Faith & Protection is the lowest KCI.

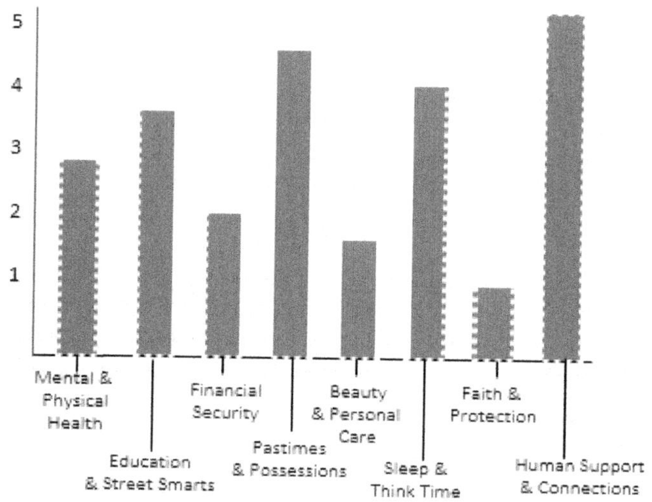

Using this Dashboard as an example, the person created the following Personal Confidence Plan:

1. Pick one KCI that you'd like to focus on first.
   e.g., Faith & Protection.
2. What is one thing (small win) you will commit to do immediately to improve your confidence?
   e.g., Call three insurance companies to get new quotes for my house coverage this week.
3. How will you know it is working (metric)?
   e.g., I will get the quotes and decide which provider to go with.

4. How will you stay accountable?

   e.g., I put a reminder in my calendar to do this and I will ask my mother to check in with me at the end of the week.

Create your own dashboard:

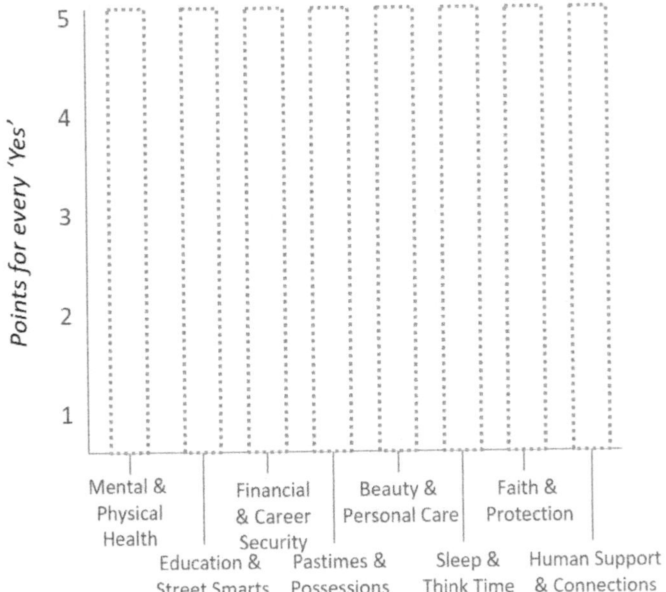

Key Confidence Indicators (KCIs)

Once you have filled in your Personal Confidence Dashboard, you should see clearly that some of your Key Confidence Indicators (KCIs) scored above 3 and some scored below. This is true for everyone—and what is high or low will change over time for each of us.

Now, build a Personal Confidence Plan:

1. Pick **one** of the KCIs where you scored lowest—if you have multiple ones at that score, pick one. It doesn't matter which one you pick first—the key is to pick one and focus on increasing it.

2. Next, look at the list on the next two pages for ideas on how you might improve that KCI. Pick **one** of the ideas or add one of your own. It's important though to pick **only** one and commit to doing that one thing.

3. Fill in your Plan and share it with your accountability partner.

The goal here is to take control of a weak KCI and find something that really works for you personally that will increase your confidence in that specific area. The action can be simple, such as getting a haircut, going to bed by 11 pm, or scheduling dinner out with friends. It is critical that the action is measurable so you know concretely when that action is done and that the goal was met like the examples above. Stating that you need to lose weight or exercise more aren't quantifiable enough without setting specific goals. Without the specific goals identified, you can't be confident of your ability to achieve or celebrate them.

Once you have that KCI score raised, you can move on to another needy KCI. Just don't try to do more than one thing at a time, and remember to celebrate small wins!

Wants Are Desired, Not Required

Wants can be practical or fantasies (yup, any and all). You may know the number of kids you want, your type of ideal house, or the kind of car you'd like to drive. You may want a different job title, to have a better spouse, or to be one. Wants are also *enablers* that allow us to live according to our values. Wants can motivate us to do things for the sake of fulfilling the want. When we have certainty about an expected, desired outcome, we are motivated to make it happen. "I am certain I want that, so I am going to do whatever it takes to get it."

When your needs and wants are clearly in alignment with your values, they act like bumpers or guidelines to your decisions. They keep us comfortable and certain about how we want/need to act, react, and interact. In New England, it is common to use brightly colored stakes to mark where the snowplow should stop so it doesn't wreck your lawn or landscaping. Those stakes are metaphorically the same: we plant stakes in our brains to help us confidently behave/decide given the boundaries of our values, needs, and wants.

Confidence Requires Constant Course Corrections

Confidence comes from making calm decisions based on having as much knowledge as reasonably possible. You can't and will never have all the desired information or experience. There may also be situations, people, or other things that you can't control that impact your mindset, attitude, and ability to think clearly. Confident people make a *good enough* decision and then move on. If more information becomes available, if they gain experience, or there are other mitigating factors, confident people consciously decide they want to adjust their prior decision so they can remain confident. They don't stay mired in past poor decisions. They examine the situation and weigh things against their values, needs, and wants. They then *choose to stay confident* by learning from the experience and changing course as necessary.

That isn't recklessness or any type of weakness. Being willing to pivot, course correct, or otherwise recognize an error is a good thing. It is virtuous humility that allows confident people to sometimes realize they made a mistake and were wrong. One of the strongest signs of confident people is their willingness to change and try different ways to achieve or acquire what they want—often despite what other people think.

Some people may see *wants* as selfish. In some cases, they may be (e.g., I want to win the lottery.) To always be confident of your decisions and behaviors, I invite you to conscientiously identify them as *wants* without turning them into *needs*. That enables confident authenticity and clarity.

Needs/Wants Test

Here is a simple method to be confident about needs and wants:

1. Be brutally honest with yourself WHY you need or want something.

2. Consider what happens if you don't have that need/want fulfilled.

3. Determine if THAT need/want is the best way to satisfy the WHY.

When you examine the real motivation and opportunity cost, you will recognize what is necessary versus what is discretionary. The goal is to be clear about why you are choosing to do or buy something. You don't have to have a quantifiable reason per se, just be clear why you need or want it. When your need or want passes the test, you gain confidence in your decision.

Example Needs/Wants Test: Buying a New Car

You see a luxury car that sings to you. You really want to buy it even though you know it will require you to take a big loan. Therefore, you try to convince yourself it is needed. Again, the objective isn't to talk yourself out of buying the car, but rather to make a conscientious, regret-free decision by managing the emotion within the decision-making process.

1: Consider why you want or need that thing.

"I really want that new car. I really need it."

Why?

"Because it will impress and attract clients and make them think that I am good at what I do."

2: What if You Don't Get it

"I won't look or feel as successful and that will be visible to clients."

3: What other ways can the need/want be satisfied?

Can I demonstrate my success in other ways without taking on significant debt?

For sure! I can get some new clothes, a new briefcase, skincare, maybe video interview past clients to prove to prospects (and to me) how I successfully helped those clients.

Being clear about *why* you need or want something makes decision-making a whole lot easier. When you tie wants/needs to your values, it justifies the otherwise unquantifiable result. The key, as you would suspect, is to be *very honest* with yourself. The other key is to be fair and compassionate. Don't justify it just because everyone else has one or does it. Don't justify it with "why not?" or "because I earned it."

All those excuses only mask that you want something because you value it. Give yourself the freedom to go after something because you want it. Just be responsible in how much time and money you spend acquiring that thing or accomplishing that goal. You can lose weight in many unhealthy or risky ways. If speed is of value to you, maybe the risks are worth it. There are always multiple ways to confidently accomplish or acquire something. Be smart and think about ways to satisfy your needs without regretting later how you did it.

Even with careful *enough* Metaconfident Thinking, sometimes our confidence is kicked off course—so much so, that we lose control of our actions or reactions. This is totally human, normal, and expected. Regaining control is what confident people do so well that often when they do fall off the track, they recover so quickly that no one else notices.

Tame Triggers

To protect your confidence, you must recognize villains and kryptonite that want to compromise it. Then, armed with simple tools, tips, and techniques, you can shield yourself against these and other potential confidence-kicking threats.

When someone is described as "comfortable in their own skin," it implies they are in control of themselves and seem confident. Review the visual characteristics of confident people from Part 1. We can *see* when someone is managing confidence in their head because it is conveyed to the outside world through their body and behaviors. Therefore, when you proactively protect your confidence from faltering, you remain in control of your behavior, too.

Managing confidence relies on our ability to avoid or deflect Amygdala triggers before they set off irrational Brain Stem behaviors. You can armor-up when you sense your confidence is under attack.

Please Don't Make Me Do That

You know that some situations can threaten confidence. The level of fear will vary among people and depend on specific circumstances, timing, and other variables. Consider situations such as public speaking, trying new foods, or changing a routine. For some, everyday activities can trigger confidence challenges such as driving on a highway, deciding what clothes to wear, or calling someone on the phone. More dire confidence-challenging situations may include dealing with a job loss, divorce, serious illness, etc.

Regardless of their seeming severity, these situations likely trigger one or more of the big three confidence fears: failure, regret, or rejection. As a result, the situations cause us to feel uncomfortable or anxious. Maybe you have at one time been emotionally depleted or paralyzed by this dynamic.

One way to deal with a confidence-challenging situation is to simply avoid it. That may not be feasible without impacting important relationships or opportunities. Avoiding things that feel risky, scary, and out of your wheelhouse can certainly be career and life-limiting. If you decide to avoid a situation, aim to be confident that it is what you want to do, despite knowing the potential impact of that decision.

A good way to help you decide if you should go or not go forward is to use the Needs/Wants Test from the last chapter. This can help you can think through the implications and options of the situation, ensuring that your values, needs, and wants are being respected.

For example, if you have a fear of public speaking, your Needs/Wants Test might look like this:

> **1: Consider why you want or need that thing (in this case, why you need or want to do something that is otherwise uncomfortable).**
>
> "I need/want to speak in public."
>
> Why?
>
> "Because it'll help my career, and I have important ideas I want to share. If I don't, I won't impress people who I can help and who can help me. I won't be a subject matter expert and I won't have an important business skill that successful people need."
>
> **2: What if you don't get it (or in this case, do the thing that is uncomfortable)?**
>
> "I may get overlooked for promotions. I won't be asked to voice my opinion or be respected when I do. I will be mad at

myself for not being able to do something that other people can."

3: What other ways can your need/want be satisfied?

"I can write papers or other communications to demonstrate my knowledge. I can support other people who are presenting. However, neither of these will be as effective as if I am presenting."

These three questions identify and organize the emotion together with analytical logic, so you make a better decision whether you need to, want to, should, or should not overcome your fear.

Inside Out Pet Peeves

An enlightening and actually fun exercise we use at ACI to discover some of the situation villains is called "Inside Out Pet Peeves."

Pet peeves are easy to access in your head. Think about something that always ticks you off. For example: Hate it when people are late? Can't stand it when someone blames other people every time something goes wrong? Want to scream when someone doesn't say thank you?

Pet peeves elicit emotional responses, so they are baked into our memory and therefore are easy to recall.

1.   Pick any one of your pet peeves, and first recognize that it is an emotional trigger. When someone does that, it makes you angry, maybe furious. That is your Amygdala telling you there is danger. The danger is a violation of your values, needs, or wants. It's like touching an electric fence; your Amygdala is letting you know that you are going outside of your personal confidence boundary. It may even feel like an electric shock. A jolt of emotion that implies something isn't right. Your Brain Stem grabs that opportunity to make you feel angry, frustrated, and offended.

Pick one of your pet peeves: "I hate it when

____."

2.   Next, take the pet peeve and flip it inside out. That is, figure out why it ticks you off by finding the value violation in it. Rephrase the sentence with "I appreciate it when....."

For example, "I hate it when people are late" turns into "I appreciate (value) when people are on time." "I can't stand it when someone always blames other people" turns into "I appreciate when people own their flaws and mistakes." "I want to scream when someone doesn't say thank you" becomes "I appreciate when someone expresses gratitude." Hopefully, you get the idea.

Restate your pet peeve: "I appreciate it when

____."

When Pet Peeves are turned inside out, you find the value nugget that explains why you get angry or sad because one of your values is not being upheld by others. While you can't necessarily change other people's behavior, you can change your response by recognizing 'anti-confidence' triggers.

When you use an Inside Out Pet Peeve, you might feel better just from understanding why your emotions were activated. You might also find an appropriate way to share that value recognition with the other person. For example, with someone who is late once but has a reasonable excuse, try to consider it as inconvenient to you, but unintentionally done by them. If they are perpetually late, don't be unnecessarily polite and tell them it is okay. Instead say something like, "I appreciate your apology since I value when people are on time."

You can even commend someone when they are respecting one of your values. "I really appreciated that you took ownership of that and didn't blame other people." Consider this brain training for the other person. Call it positive reinforcement, imprinting, or behavioral conditioning—let others know your values so they can learn to respect them.

Not everyone, will respond as you desire. If someone is perpetually late without any remorse, it's hard not to get angry. Let them know authentically that it is important to you when you schedule the next meeting. You could say: "The past times we met, we got started very late. With all the commitments we both have, I would appreciate if we could start our meetings on time." (Note the word *we* here so you don't trigger their caveperson defensiveness.)

If this type of comment is awkward for you or otherwise directed at someone who has authority, you may need to just readjust your expectations. You can't change their behavior, but you don't have to join them or otherwise feel slighted. Remember that other people may not share your values. They may also have legitimate reasons for the way they behave. Don't assume they are doing it maliciously, intentionally, or in any way to specifically disrespect you. They are simply not aligned with your values, needs, and wants.

Who Are You Allergic To?

We all have certain people and/or certain types of people that emotionally intimidate us. Some scare us because they are mean or arrogant. Others are notably smarter, more accomplished, or simply *better* than we are in some way. You feel uncomfortable, jittery, and awkward. You may verbally stumble, giggle, or do other things that indicate nervousness when you are around them. Realize that the person isn't the problem; your response is. You are not proactively deflecting or managing that fear-based Amygdala trigger.

Recall our earlier discussion about Confidence Imposters and Bonehead Behaviors. Those are confidence killers because they are forms of bullying (intentional or not) that make one person feel inferior so the other can feel relatively superior. The bully wants to dominate or be the center of attention. Regardless of the cause or intent, they can trigger us to behave in ways that we are later likely to regret.

Specific people who challenge my confidence:

To deal with these types of people, here are two simple techniques:

1.   Notice when someone makes you feel nervous. (My ACI co-founder, Lynnette, calls it *feeling emotionally itchy*, like having an allergic reaction.) Then stop and *brainmark* that moment in your head. Catalog that person in your "Someone Who Makes Me Feel Not Confident" file. You can try to minimize interaction with that person, or at least come prepared whenever you know you will meet or talk with him/her. Give your brain and behavior a *heads up* so they are ready with protective shields. Proactively decide to be confident in their presence. Maybe you could talk less to avoid opening doors for the villain. You could even restrict your responses to mostly yes/no answers. Most importantly, stay mindful that the other person is the one lacking confidence—not you!

2.   Label the behavior. Say inside your head, "He is trying to be the smartest person in the room," or "She's talking over me." Labeling requires metaconfident thought that invokes the Prefrontal Cortex to act and be in control. It has a similar effect as breathing or using a focal point. You give your Prefrontal Cortex control by actively thinking about someone else's behavior. You overtake the Brain Stem caveperson-response associated with frustration or fear. By naming the other person's behavior, you control the otherwise emotional reaction and intelligently analyze it so you can remain in a confident zone. Take the brain's high, rational road and simply witness the other person's caveperson-like, confidence descent.

Not Just a Person, but Those Types

Maybe your confidence gets intimidated not just by specific people, but by a category of them. For example, when I was little, I was afraid of one of my grandparent's friends. He was a gregarious guy who would put his face close to mine, and terrified me with his big, black, lip-brow of a mustache. At that time, every man with a mustache would freak me out. Thankfully I outgrew that fear since many of my now-favorite men are handsomely mustached, including my husband and oldest son!

Maybe you act differently when you are around very smart or highly credentialed people. Do scientists, engineers, doctors, or other professionals cause you to feel less confident about your own capabilities—even if you are one yourself? How about aggressive, loud, or expressive individuals? Is there some archetype that you know makes you feel weak or scared? How about celebrities, relatives, or higher ups? Can you identify what types and why?

Types of people who challenge my confidence:

When you know the types, you can apply the same two suggestions offered to handle specific trigger people that were presented earlier. First, recognize the type, and then second, label the type in your mind. Use the emotional warning alert to trigger some Metaconfident Thinking and deliberately think through and decide how you want to react. Don't just pray that the earth will open and swallow you up. Recognize your cognitive allergic reaction and label the behavior to give yourself a protective shot of confidence.

They're Human Just Like You

Perhaps the most powerful and simple tip is to humanize villains: remember that anyone who challenges your confidence is human, just like you.*

Their brains and bodies operate just like yours. They have their own insecurities and challenges—though sometimes theirs are less visible or better managed than your own. Imposters and Boneheads are trying to fake and steal confidence, but it only works with people who are not confident enough to protect their own confidence. You are as humanly entitled to be confident as anyone else.

*(*We must acknowledge that there are some sociopathic and border personalities that do not operate with the same ethics, intentions, or possibly neurological constructs as others. How and why these individuals are this way is outside our scope except to note that we are likely to interact at some point with people who will not act in accordance to what we construe as humane, polite, or rational.)*

Even as a master of Metaconfident Thinking, there will still be times when you don't have the ability/energy/time to control confidence well. We may act, react, or interact in ways that aren't congruent to our values, needs, and wants. We may do things that we regret or aren't reflecting who we want to be. When this happens, we need quick and easy ways to override the autonomic responses to cope with confidence emergencies.

Override Autonomic Responses

Even with well-conditioned confidence, there will be times when our protective shields are penetrated, and someone or something triggers an unwanted behavioral response. Confident people have ways to quickly recover.

Villains will inevitably find a way to get through and rattle your confidence. It may be because you are tired, misjudged a situation, or trustingly let your guard down. Even when you master Metaconfident Thinking, you may be unable to control an unwanted Brain Stem reaction.

Autonomic overrides can help you handle the temporary confidence crisis faster and more efficiently. When your confidence is kicked off-track, there are some very simple techniques to get it realigned.

Mind Your Breath

Any type of yoga or martial art uses mindful breathing as a key method to maintain your focus and presence. It not only fuels your muscles, it strengthens your mind, too.

Try it now. Breathe deeply and slowly, ideally through your nose. Inhale and hold for a second, then exhale through your mouth. You have just used your Prefrontal Cortex to overtake the normally autonomic Brain Stem function of breathing.

Plus, when we are unnerved, we often don't *remember* to breathe—essentially, we unknowingly hold our breath in fright. Our brains need oxygen to function, let alone be able to make confident decisions.

This metaconfident technique is so deceivingly simple that we don't *think* to do it but should whenever an emotional trigger is activated.

Anytime you feel anxious, frustrated, or otherwise uncomfortable, mindfully breathe.

Balance Your Brain and Your Body Will Follow

Another common yoga technique is using a focal point. Focal points have the same effect as conscious breathing: they give the Prefrontal Cortex control. When you are holding a yoga position, your Amygdala senses discomfort, failure to get into, or the inability to hold, a position. You may even worry about the potential embarrassment of falling over. Wobbling or reaching for something stable to hold are physical responses activated by your Brain Stem trying to *protect* you. When you consciously give control to your calmer Prefrontal Cortex, you can reduce the Brain Stem's defensive impact.

Here is a simple, 1-minute way to prove that you can take control of your brain:

1.   Stand with your feet in tandem, one in front of the other (see picture below). It may be a little difficult to balance but try without holding onto anything around you.

2.   While keeping your feet in tandem, *close your eyes* for 15 seconds and continue to balance. Then come back to reading this. Ready?

     Was it harder to balance? For most people, it is.

3.   Now, keeping your feet in tandem and eyes open, find a *focal point.* Any spot or thing at eye level in front of you will

work. Really stare at the focal point and then notice how much more stable your body is.

4.   The final step is to keep your feet in tandem and again, close your eyes and continue to try to balance for 15 seconds. But this time, continue to try to *see* the focal point through your eyelids. Force your brain to focus on the focal point. After the 15 seconds, return here. Ready?

One, two, three, close your eyes but still *focus* (for 15 seconds, then come back to read).

Bet it was easier to balance this time—even with your eyes closed.

Why?

This simple exercise proves that when you control your thoughts by deliberately directing your focus, your body follows. Because your brain was busy thinking about the visual focal point, you put the energy and activity in your Prefrontal Cortex—where all your rational, logical, and more controlled thinking is. You removed the worry of potentially falling over, and the subsequent autonomic wobbly body response that your Brain Stem triggers.

Communication Is Confidence's BFF

Writing and talking are also powerful ways to use your executive functions and exercise the Prefrontal Cortex. Communication utilizes the logical, calculative parts of your Prefrontal Cortex to assemble proper sentences and string together meaningful words. Invoking these skills requires Prefrontal Cortex action.

Some people enjoy journaling or other forms of private expression. These are perfectly legit. Any form of communicating works—even if you aren't communicating directly with anyone else. Expressing feelings forces you to use your conscious brain.

For some people or in some circumstances, it can be more effective to communicate with another person. You can seek out a professional life/business/executive coach, mentor, psychologist, or friend—essentially, anyone who is a good, active listener. The best *thought partners* don't put words in your mouth or give advice, but rather facilitate your thought process by asking questions and being non-judgmental. We'll get into this more in our final chapter on Coaching Confidence.

Stereotypically, women tend to be more comfortable expressing feelings than men. However, not all females are comfortable opening up, while some males truly enjoy it. Don't be discouraged if you can't express your thoughts easily. There are other ways to express your emotions. For example, art, music, or sports may be better outlets for you. Yet, those don't typically obtain the same communication goal of finding a specific way to proactively take control of your thoughts and feelings.

Plan Not to Panic

I joke that my name (Alyssa) starts and ends with a Type A. That is not necessarily a good or bad trait. I have turned that into one of my superpowers: I'm a planning pro. This means, I'm good at thinking through steps and requirements ahead of time. It means I'm good at organizing things and seeing an optimal order of operations as well as dependencies. It also means I identify required deadlines, resources, contingencies, and systems needed to deliver quality results. Planning is an asset, but it can also become a liability.

My own husband is an uber-planner. In the past, he planned everything to calm his anxiety and gain more control of future activities, tasks, travel—anything new, important, or forecastable. He likes order and predictability. It's one of the reasons he became a teacher. He knows what to teach for the entire year thanks to curriculums and state frameworks. We used to tease him for being too prepared—to a point where nothing was spontaneous or flexible. While we were thankful when he got things done efficiently, without hassle or unexpected cost, any change of plan would cause him to be in a foul mood and be unpleasant to be around, often unbearable. Maybe you are or you know someone just like that, too?

The challenge for everyone, is to not let the plan control our emotions. For my husband, his need to plan would trigger his anxiety. He would get visibly frustrated and even mean when a plan didn't manifest as he envisioned. His behavior would then make everyone else uncomfortable and unhappy.

Planning is powerful, as it invokes Metaconfident Thinking. It allows us to think proactively and prepare our brains for situations that may challenge our confidence. We also need to recognize when a plan *causes* fear of failure or regret, rather than *alleviates* it. Lack of a complete plan or unforeseen changes to a well-thought-out plan can trigger a Brain Stem, caveperson-like reaction. Thankfully my husband overcame his planning inflexibility and can now very effectively manage a plan—and his Amygdala.

Shiny Notification Syndrome

Mental multiprocessing is a myth since your brain cannot focus on two things at the same time. It shifts from one thing to the next, sometimes so quickly back and forth that you *think* you are doing both at the same time.[48] Even if you can effectively pat your head and simultaneously rub your tummy, it is because you are shifting between neurons quickly enough that your body doesn't change course. And while this is an entertaining human skill, when we constantly switch focus, we use up brain resources.

When you are working on something like writing a report or email while being distracted by notifications and other seemingly relevant interruptions, you don't realize that you are wasting valuable brain fuel. Each time you get pinged, you decide (consciously or not) if you should pay attention to the interruption. As a result, you are likely to get less done and/or at a lower quality. You are probably more tired when you are done, too, from all that brain load balancing.

Some people can manage background distraction like music or the TV. They use it almost like white noise to calm their brains without making it a focused distraction. Other people need complete quiet to work, focus, or sleep. Your results may vary depending on many factors. Bottom line: constant disruption isn't good. Try to turn off notifications and other controllable distractions to optimize cognitive resources.

Thinking Time Outs

You already know that exercise is good for your body and you may even know it is good for mental health, too. Exercise provides blood flow to your brain to fuel it just like your muscles. When you exercise, you also give your brain a mini vacation since you are doing less intensive intellectual thinking as you focus on the physical activity.

Brain Breaks

Another way to keep your brain fully powered is to work in sprints. New studies show that for most people, they optimize mental work productivity by doing 60-90 minutes of intellectual work (such as writing, analysis, organizational, etc.) followed by a short break.[49] Any type of break can help, especially any form of exercise. The physical activity not only gets blood and oxygen flowing, but you are deciding to reboot your Prefrontal Cortex, giving temporary control to your less brilliant Brain Stem.

Depending on what you're doing and where you are, you might not want to break a sweat or raise your heartbeat. Walking away from your desk to get a cup of coffee, calling someone on the phone, even playing a game can effectively hand the thinking baton to another part of your brain and give the depleted brain cells and pathways time to refresh. When you push through longer intense thinking periods, you essentially tire those pathways and ultimately invite in the biggest confidence killer of all: being tired.

You may recognize my play on words in the subtitle here. In Hamilton, Aaron Burr advises Alexander Hamilton to be a better statesman by talking less and smiling more.[50] It's excellent confidence advice. Still even better advice would have been to talk less and sleep more. It's hard to be smart (or smile) when you are exhausted. As discussed previously, tiredness is the ultimate kryptonite to confidence, since our brain conserves its limited resources for critical functions. As a result, it slows your neural synapses and weakens your ability to manage villains and other triggers.

While you can't always get enough sleep or control the quality of your sleep, you can at least recognize when you are tired. Make a mental note that your fuel level is low and try to conserve what you have. Proactively go into *safe mode* and slow down your mouth and decisions. To avoid saying, driving, or doing something else you might regret, slow down and give your brain more time to think. And yes, Aaron Burr's advice helps, too. Smiling can neurologically help you to feel and appear more confident, too.[51]

Make Confident Decisions

We already noted in Part 2 that diplomatic decisiveness is a recognized confidence characteristic. People who waffle or defer to other people's decisions aren't considered confident.

Included in the 35,000 daily decisions Google says we make, are choices such as what time to wake up, what to eat all day long, what to wear, and which posts to "like." Some decisions are easy, while others tax our brain. Easier decisions have clearer implications. Harder decisions test our values, resolve, and resourcefulness. Our confidence dictates every decision—even if we decide that we are not confident.

A confident mindset recognizes that:

- Not all decisions will result in ideal outcomes, even with conclusive evidence.
- Not deciding can be worse than the potential outcomes of making a wrong decision.
- Not learning from a bad decision is the only bad decision.

Knowing how to make confident decisions is a critical career and life skill, even when there isn't ideal information.

Learning how to make better decisions requires training your Prefrontal Cortex to take in and analyze all types of information. Some of the data may be quantitative and seemingly objective. Some data will inevitably be subjective, qualitative, or maybe just gut feelings. Like any skill, the more you make *good enough* decisions, the more confident you will become, especially if you are mindful about learning and improving each time. Whether this creates neuroplastic changes in our brains, or not, almost doesn't matter. You gain confidence from knowing you have the competence to make good decisions.

Comparisons Can Create Confidence

Like computer-enabled artificial intelligence, we naturally train our brains the same way by pattern matching with existing knowledge and experiences. When we are presented with new information, we apply what we already know to understand, categorize, and file the fresh data appropriately. When we are presented with a decision, we then refer to that dataset to help us make a confident decision. Consider anytime you've caught yourself thinking, "this is just like…" You are matching the new information with the knowledge you already have so you can decide with confidence what to think, decide, and do next.

Anytime we mindfully learn, we automatically search for a comparison of something that we already know to use as the foundation for that learning. Therefore, our experiences, biases, national and organizational culture, plus our personal and group aspirations create many filters. This makes human decision more often unpredictable and uncontrollable. A confident decision will be right for that person given the data, personal filters, and situational variables that were there *at that time.*

As we have described throughout this book, a confident decision is defined as one that is *within the boundaries of an individual's values, needs, and wants.* Therefore, even with having objective, perceived conclusive data, someone may not heed the calculated direction in favor of following their heart. That person's decision dataset supports their own values, needs, and wants—at that point in time. Their confident decision may seem irrational to someone else who has different filters and seemingly more rational judgement.

Decide to Decide

Many would argue that human decision-making isn't as optimal as a computer's ability, since machines perform more reliably, methodically, and objectively. Mind you, this doesn't mean computers make *better* decisions than humans; computers can make *faster* ones. Depending on the decision, being human gives us critical data that a computer cannot collect or compute. *Subjective data* is information that we feel, sense, or believe. In many personal decision-making scenarios, we should seek out this qualitative information. Like a pilot having radar but not the visibility to confidently land a plane, if you don't use subjective data, your own decision-making ability can be compromised. You may see the runway where you want to land, but unless you pay attention to your own turbulence, you may be blown off your confidence course.

For example, maybe you've always wanted to start a business, but it is a hard decision to make given your current employee salary, benefits, and years of experience. At least financially, the data doesn't support your entrepreneurial idea. You write a business case, research the market, and even do some testing, but the data still doesn't add up to financially justify the change. Yet you know, despite the numbers, you really are yearning to do this new business. It's pulling at you as a daily distraction and it's demotivating you to do your current job well. Staying in your job means you are deciding to transgress your own values, needs, and wants. It is hard to argue with the seemingly rational decision to stay in your job. The subjective data is telling you otherwise. Eventually, the denial creates disengagement, maybe even depression. It certainly impacts your well-being and overall confidence.

Timing Is Everything, Including an Excuse

I'm sure you've said more than once, "Timing is everything." I bet you've also used it as an excuse at least once to avoid or postpone a decision. Too often we use *timing* to quell our gut feeling to say we'll do something when the time is right. In this way, we defer a decision to another time when it may be easier or more clearly aligned to our values, needs, and wants.

In some cases, we recognize that we are not ready to make a confident decision. Maybe we need more time to think, gather data, gain experience, or grow emotionally. Without the necessary information or situation, deferring a decision may truly be the confident best choice. Just be sure that the postponement won't cause more negative impact than making an immediate, imperfect decision. We live in agile times that applaud us for moving forward fast, being open to future insight, and altering the path. This course correction process overcomes decision paralysis and waiting for the perfect moment to decide. The world moves fast, so waiting for the right time may be the wrong decision for no other reason than there is rarely an optimal right time.

Decision Game Plan

Sometimes we drag our feet or simply don't want to decide because we fear failure, regret, or rejection. Admittedly, some types of decisions are not that easy to think about and plan, such as high stakes, subjective career, or relationship decisions. Other decisions certainly benefit from unbiased, factual data.

If you are stuck fearing a decision's potential personal consequences, it is helpful to plan how and when you are going to decide. By consciously committing to get the decision done, it takes away some of the fear, guilt, or possible shame about deferring a decision.

Creating a Decision Game Plan can help remove some of the emotional inertia from making an uncomfortable decision. Think of a Decision Game Plan as a form of *Metadecision Thinking.* You are deciding how and when you will decide.

With all decisions, ideally, we want to be as aware as possible of biases and other filters we may have. We also need to honor subjective data—how we feel or what we believe to be right according to our values, needs, and wants. Better than pros and cons, which discount our emotions, a Decision Game Plan helps balance apparent facts with relevant feelings.

A Decision Game Plan doesn't have to be fancy or even written (though it is recommended). Like with the previously discussed Personal Confidence Plan, any plan is more likely to happen when you have accountability baked in. Tell someone else about the plan and/or post it somewhere that you can easily view to remind yourself of the decision schedule.

Decision Game Plans should be realistic and specific. They should argue why the decision and timing is important—as well as the risks and rewards if you do or don't make the decision on time...or don't make it at all.

Decision Game Plan Outline:

- Why is this decision important to me?

- When do I need to make this decision and what happens if I don't make it on time?

- Why am I worried about making this decision?

- What information do I need (require) to make an *educated-enough* decision?

- How will I feel when I make the decision?

Example Decision Game Plan: Deciding if You Should Buy Your First House

- **Why is this decision important to me?**

  "I hate paying rent that doesn't seem to financially benefit me in the short or long term. I want to invest in something that provides equity and tax benefits. Owning a house is something that I dream about and will feel proud about."

- **When do I need to make this decision and what happens if I don't make it on time?**

"There isn't a deadline per se but the sooner I decide, the better for my mental well-being and potentially my financial situation. I'd like to make the decision before the end of this year. If I don't decide by then, I may miss out on the opportunity to get the house or type of house I would like due to competitive bidders, not presenting financial readiness at the time of offer, or loan interest rates potentially going up. This will make me feel sad and disappointed in myself. I will have to remain in my apartment and may lose the benefits and pride of home ownership."

- **Why am I worried about making this decision?**

"I may pay too much for a house and then not be able to afford it or sell it to recoup my investment. Worse yet, I may find a better house after and regret the one I bought."

- **What information do I need to make an *educated-enough* decision?**

"I should understand home values in the past, present, and estimated future within the market that I am considering. Also, I need to know what I can afford and what's involved in getting a loan.

I will talk to one or two agents and research the market to get a sense of the home values and available inventory. I will also contact two banks to get information about rates, loan processes, and costs. Lastly, I can calculate the cost of buying a house (utilities, taxes, insurance, etc.) versus renting for the next few years. I also need to consider moving costs, repairs, and any new furnishings I will need in the home.

All of this data will allow me to calculate the monthly payments so I will know how much I can afford."

- **How will I feel when I make the decision on time?**

> "I will feel liberated from this looming decision. If I do buy a house, I will enjoy the space and accomplishment. If I don't purchase a house, it will be for good reasons and it will help me feel better about staying in my rented apartment."

Listen to Your Gut

Not all information is concrete or correct. Even experts make mistakes, don't know everything in their space, or don't realize their own biases. Just because they learned it one way doesn't mean there aren't other, equally correct ways. Everyone knows that statistics and research can bend truth to support something we want to be true. Experts aren't any different. Whether they are quoting or creating research, remember that experts are human, too. They can usually find credentialed reasons to support why their opinions are right—myself included!

I'll even go out on a limb to say that the more *expert* someone is, the more committed to and protective of their knowledge base they are. As a result, many experts are noticeably arrogant, insecure, and difficult to interact with. They carry so much Imposter Syndrome that their caveperson Brain Stem is always in charge. And yes, I'm talking about respected experts, not just overconfident individuals who falsely believe they are experts.

One of the saddest effects of having your Brain Stem in the driver seat is that you're likely to be unable to be innovative or open to new ideas which could improve your expertise and overall decision-making. I bet you know people like this:

They are so comfortable taking the one, tried and true road, that they won't even consider going another more scenic and perhaps, more efficient route. They know the existing, learned path works and gives them confidence. They don't allow anyone to 'move their cheese' or challenge their expertise. They think they are growth-minded, but they are only interested in building on the existing foundation they already have. They may aim to learn new things, but they will never challenge the things they already know. They need those things to be right, to be true. Their ego and career can't handle the disappointment if they were to find out otherwise. If they aren't an expert in that area, then what are they?

Or does this apply to you? We can all see ourselves in the above description to some extent. It feels like we have confidence because of our expertise but I hope you see now—expertise doesn't guarantee confidence; in fact, it often challenges it.

Experts' blinders are a very sad result of a lack of core confidence. In my own experience, these blinders prevent doctors, engineers, financial advisors, and other very smart people from doing the right things and making optimal decisions. They confuse confidence with ego and protect the latter at the cost of the former.

Confidence Begets Confidence

While we all want to make confident decisions, an equally important measurement is how we also enable others to make confident decisions. An employer wants to be confident about a new hire's ability to do the job just as much as the new hire's confidence wants to get it done. A great doctor gives his/her patients confidence knowing they are in confident medical hands.

Beyond bedside manner, giving other people confidence requires a lot more data than just reading vitals or test results. It requires emotional intelligence as well as real-time situational and self-awareness. Therefore, some of the decision-making data will always be subjective, subconscious, and/or unquantifiable. It is critical information that is within our brains which we often don't acknowledge is important to our decision process. This subconscious data can save careers and lives—especially our own.

I am optimistic that there is movement to respect subjective data to help us feel and function better. There are dozens of respected medical professionals who profess that your brain is unconsciously taking in and analyzing all sorts of subjective data. The brain then tries to organize and make sense of the data in our dreams, subconscious, and other covert cognitive processes.

As if you needed yet another reason to sleep beyond what I have written already, our dreams help us access information that may be beyond our conscious reach. When we sleep, we remove the distraction and restraint of our required daily thinking. Our resting brains are disarmed, unencumbered, and able to access more cognitive resources to fully analyze what we are feeling relative to our values, needs, and wants. No wonder we often wake up with decision clarity. Our brain was hard at work while we were sleeping and running background processes so it could make a fully confident decision.

When you find it hard to fall asleep because your brain is buzzing, it may be because you are fixated on some misaligned information. You might possibly find yourself thinking in circles or consistently losing the thread of a thought. The anxiety makes it hard to shut your brain and body down, which then doesn't allow for the brain to do its subconscious-inclusive thinking. When we don't or can't sleep, we deprive ourselves of a necessary part of the thinking, decision-making, and confidence cycle. Sleeping is not just scheduled maintenance or cleaning. It gives our brain time to defrag, upgrade, and audit all the current data. All that work happens off-hours when you aren't *in production* of behaviors and your brain can afford the mental resources needed to focus on the total cognitive data—both conscious AND subconscious.

Stress Is a Signal

A tired brain also amplifies stress. Small issues can appear insurmountable, more dire. Tired, stressed brains may cause us to be overly sensitive, angry, disappointed, frustrated, and unnecessarily pissed off.

In fact, stressed brains can cause serious physical harm. Some say stress is one of our biggest human killers causing heart attacks, neuropathies, and other serious conditions. We all want to reduce stress, especially in our overwhelming modern world. Stress can be used for good. As I previously explained, when operating at peak performance, elite athletes use signs of stress to fuel positive, productive feelings. They recognize stress as a warning and take control of that information to proactively decide how to behave.

Consider this: being excited has the same biological results as being nervous. Whether you are being presented with an honor or scared by a horror movie, your heart may beat faster, you may also feel flush and jittery. Similar neurotransmitters are released such that it is up to your brain to decide how to use that behavioral activation to trigger feeling either exuberant or scared.

Think about stress as a way in which your brain is screaming for your attention. Your brain knows that something is not right, and you aren't dealing with it enough or properly. Maybe you are avoiding an important decision, or you made a decision that goes against your values, needs, or wants. Your brain wants you to fix things, and if you ignore that alert, it will recruit other parts of your body until you pay attention and do what is needed. Persistently ignored emotional stress can create tension-related symptoms and life-impacting conditions such as back or joint and muscle pain, headaches, and exhaustion. Stress is a notorious cause of reflux, hemorrhoids, and a bunch of other inconvenient ailments.[52] Unsurprisingly, stress makes it difficult to think clearly and make confident decisions.

While we can't practically remove everyday stress from our lives, we can learn to handle it better. One way is to identify it, embrace it as an alarm, and commit to dealing with the cause. I realize this is easier to type than do, especially when there is a lot on the line such as a career or relationship decisions. Anytime you can sense one of the confidence fears of failure, regret, or rejection kicking in, those can cause stress and/or be amplified by stress. Taking control of that stress signal as soon as possible can enable you to use the stress more productively, even fueling your motivation to more mindfully commit to making a confident decision sooner than later.

Big Life Decision Checklist

To help acknowledge and factor in subjective, emotional data that can create stress, there is a helpful ACI tool called, "The Big Life Decision Checklist." When faced with a significant decision, there are inevitable financial and emotional parts to consider. There may be legal, political, and social aspects as well. Talking through the options with a spouse, friend, or coach can be very helpful. Writing down pros and cons can also organize your thoughts. As you now know, emotional data muddles our decision-making,[53] but we need to pay attention to it. When we are clear about both the logic and emotion involved, we make more conscientious, confident decisions.

Big Decision:
Why am I doing this?
What happens if I don't?
How will I feel when I do?
Decision Due Date (if known):

Key Decision Questions	Do I have:	What is required to ensure this?	What do I need to get clarity or address this?
COMPETENCE *Can I do it (well enough)?*	☐ Knowledge ☐ Experience ☐ Current Ability	Self & Social Awareness	
VALUES *Do I want to do it (enough)?*	☐ Motivation ☐ Priority ☐ Direction	Identified Purpose & Desire	
BELIEFS *Do I have (enough) faith that undesirable potential outcomes are unlikely?*	☐ Low risk of failure ☐ Low risk of rejection ☐ Low risk of regret	Clear Direction & Plan	
SUPPORT *Do I have what's needed to do it well (enough)?*	☐ Necessary assets (financial, materials, etc.) ☐ Necessary people (e.g. on my team or around me) ☐ Conducive environment (e.g. economic, political)	Communication & Accountability	

Example Big Life Decision Checklist: New Job

Big Decision: *Should I apply for the opportunity posted at the other company?*
Why am I doing this? *I could potentially make more money.*
What happens if I don't? *I stay where I am and make enough money but not as much as I would like.*
How will I feel when I do? *Proud and excited to have more money to spend and share with my family.*
Decision Due Date (if known): *If I don't do this very quickly, I will lose out to other candidates.*

Key Decision Questions	Do I have:	What is required to ensure this?	What do I need to get clarity or address this?
COMPETENCE *Can I do it (well enough)?*	✓ Knowledge ✓ Experience ✓ Current Ability	Self & Social Awareness	I have three years of positive performance reviews and over ten LinkedIn recommendations. I am certified in my role and keep sharp by attending industry events.
VALUES *Do I want to do it (enough)?*	✓ Motivation ✓ Priority ✓ Direction	Identified Purpose & Desire	I can afford a good lifestyle on my current salary, but I would like to save more money for my kids' college and my own retirement.
BELIEFS *Do I have (enough) faith that undesirable potential outcomes are unlikely?*	✓ Low risk of failure ✓ Low risk of rejection ☐ Low risk of regret	Clear Direction & Plan	I worry that the new company and culture will not be as good as my current one. Therefore, I need to talk to some employees at the new place and read comments on Glassdoor.
SUPPORT *Do I have what's needed to do it well (enough)?*	✓ Necessary assets (financial, materials, etc.) ☐ Necessary people (e.g. on my team or around me) ✓ Conducive environment (e.g. economic, political)	Communication & Accountability	It is a good economic time to change jobs with market demand high. I also have been doing my job for a while and haven't been told about a planned promotion or raise. I will ask my current company to see what they can offer.

When making big decisions, asking for other people's input can be a great help. It can provide you with information or perspective you didn't have that enables a better decision. Soliciting other people's input may open some unforeseeable cans of worms—things you need to be aware of and proactively manage.

If you ask for their input, listen to it. Don't deflect it or otherwise discount it. You don't have to agree, but you should acknowledge and consider their advice. Just remember that other people's opinions can be tainted by their own lack of confidence, jealousy, or ignorance. Biases, experiences, education, and many other factors will slant someone's perspective about your situation.

If you ask multiple people at the same time for decision input, you may cause Groupthink. Groupthink can be helpful if you are trying to give confidence to individuals who otherwise may not join or accept your opinion on their own. The peer pressure of the group can help sway or support the group's best interest. Groupthink can be an extremely negative, counterproductive, and inaccurate way to gain feedback. Ask any focus group facilitator. People's original opinions can be easily swayed or even manipulated by other stronger members in that group. As such, beware of getting personal feedback from a group that may not really be reflecting the true perspective of the individuals had they not been in the group discussion.

And most certainly, don't discount your own expertise and experience. Only you know the entire story surrounding your decision. Be confident in your own confident decision-making ability!

Part 4: COMMUNICATE

Conveying Confidence

Communication is an enormous topic unto itself. It includes written, oral, and non-verbal forms of interacting with other people. Culture, both organizationally and nationally, impacts communication, as do age, gender, and other demographics. Therefore, we will present only a few key aspects of communication here which pertain specifically to American-based confidence.

People always ask me for tips on how to act more confidently. The keyword here is "act" because everyone knows and hates fakers. You can walk or talk in a confident manner, but unless your values, needs, and wants are clear in your head, your body won't be able to fake confidence in any of your life roles. This is true even for Oscar-winning actors. Unless they are a confident person in real life, they can't portray it on stage or screen.

Therefore, this may be very harsh, but it is an honest warning: the following tips *only work if you've done the foundational confidence work first.* Biases and social expectations may also make it difficult to communicate with true confidence. This chapter is designed to give you more awareness and practical techniques to convey confidence in the various ways we as humans communicate.

Your Eyes Are Louder Than Your Mouth

Dr. Albert Mehrabian, author of "Silent Messages," conducted several studies on non-verbal communication. He found that 7% of any message is conveyed through words, 38% through certain vocal elements, and 55% through nonverbal elements (facial expressions, gestures, posture, etc.).[54] While his findings have been debated, regardless of the accuracy of his percentages, there is no doubt that non-verbal forms of communication are at least as significant as the words we exchange.

On top of the non-verbal list of confidence communication tools we have is eye contact—especially in Western cultures.[55] Our eyes convincingly convey sincerity and confidence. When we look at other people while *they are talking*, it conveys that we care about what they are saying. When we look at them while *we are talking*, it conveys we want to be connected to them. Our eyes don't let us hide the true intention of words or thoughts.

Someone who has poor eye contact is flagged as being shy, insecure, uncomfortable, or arrogant. To the person not being looked at, they can feel that they aren't being listened to and they don't matter. When you don't look at someone you're interacting with in person or even via a video call, the lack of perceived attention weakens their confidence. Therefore, having *good eye contact* is a critical confidence characteristic for you and everyone with whom you communicate.

What Does "Good Eye Contact" Really Mean?

Staring or boring a visual hole in someone is intimidating, while looking past them to the side, or over them, is disrespectful. Respectful of the many internet opinions, ACI defines good, confident eye contact as looking at someone in a friendly, non-intense way and conveying a message of engagement with your eyes. Confident eye contact welcomes other people into the conversation. It communicates genuine and visible interest in their participation and presence. Your eyes let them know *with confidence* that they matter to you.

If you are not looking at a person, and instead thinking about your next sentence or some other thought, your eyes rat you out. The same thing happens when you say or do something that you aren't confident about. Shakira says hips don't lie[56]—neither do eyes.

This is one major reason why confidence or a lack of it is so visibly apparent, even in the absence of words. We can see confidence on someone in their posture, their movement, and most of all, in their eyes. Well-intended individuals take classes and join clubs to become more effective presenters or leaders, and to improve their executive presence. They are taught the physical motions, facial expressions, and words that are associated with confidence, but their eyes *say* otherwise.

We actively and habitually look for confidence in other people's eyes and decide instantly if we think they are confident. That is why video is so popular. Seeing someone's eyes helps us decide if we should be confident in them.

They say eyes are the window to the soul. They are also the open door into your confidence.

Even with friendly eye contact, looking at someone directly for an extended period of time becomes awkward and uncomfortable. There is no real rule or scientific answer to how long you should look directly at someone. Rather than set a timer or process, use your eye contact to get and give information between you and the other person(s). Observe their body and facial movements as data points to monitor their level of confidence. Especially if you notice someone is nervous and having a hard time looking back at you, try to send them some compassion using your eyes. This can help you both can feel more comfortable, trusted, and connected.

In North America, it is customary to engage with our eyes while talking with other people. Realize that another person may not be looking back at you because of their cultural difference. In their culture, it may be considered very rude and improper to look at some people, depending on gender, rank, or other social variables. Given this potential difference in what is considered appropriate eye contact, ACI recommends looking at the people you are speaking to, even if they can't or don't want to look back at you. Be respectful of their cultural or social values, but also manage your own confidence by using your eyes to warmly invite others to visually communicate.

Your Face Is Talking Too

Your facial expression also exposes whether you are confident. An angry face diminishes everyone's confidence (e.g., the confidence imposter "perpetually pissed"), while someone without visual emotion is equally off-putting (indifferent or bored).

A genuine smile is an invaluable way to engage other people and set both their and your mindset in a productive place. There are no set rules here either except avoiding a fake or forced smile. Think about how you can support your verbal messaging by using your face to welcome, engage, and connect with people you are visually interacting with online or in person. If you show some excitement or enjoyment while interacting with that person, it is another way to convey that they matter to you. A welcoming greeting can start off a conversation much more respectfully. Smiling, nodding, or shaking your head at times, and otherwise confirming you are engaged can disarm a bad attitude and give all parties a more confident mindset. Be like a dog and wag your face a little more— it's hard to be mean to someone who is so clearly happy to be with you.

Mom Was Right—Shoulders Back

Perhaps the best recognized confidence signal is standing and sitting with your shoulders comfortably back. Study after study has proven that standing/sitting tall is a top confidence characteristic.[57]

Being stiffly straight is intimidating, and any sort of rounding of the shoulders suggests someone is lacking confidence. A closed body position with arms or hands crossed in front or behind the body implies that you are protecting yourself.[58] Standing/sitting tall is not just good for your back and abdominal muscles, it helps your confidence ones, too.

Bend It Like Beckham

Nervous energy shown through fidgeting or twitching can also convey a lack of confidence. A person may pace or sway while standing up, swivel in his chair, twirl her hair, bounce a knee, or tap the desk. Sometimes the movements are unavoidable as a result of a neurological condition. Other than for medical or other truly uncontrollable reasons, most people don't realize they are fidgeting. They also likely don't realize the impact the fidgeting has on other people. In truth, regardless of the reason or understanding, fidgeting can communicate a lack of confidence.

One way noted earlier to avoid undesired movements while you are standing is to use a *Ready Position*. This is the technique that athletes use to steady their bodies by literally grounding their physical balance to also focus their minds. It is one of the many speaker techniques I suggest to my Pitch workshop students to help calm their nerves. Ready Position can be used in front of or behind a podium. It can even be used when sitting down if you are in a meeting or on a panel. Just put your hands on the desk/table so you can see them; you'll be less tempted to tap or fidget in plain sight. If you're a swiveler, lock your chair in position or pick one that doesn't swing or roll. Knee-bouncers should sit cross-legged which makes it more difficult to bounce unknowingly.

Subservient Language & Upticks

There are several phrases that diminish our verbal contributions. Examples include:

- "This is going to sound crazy, but…"

- "This is just my opinion, but…"

- "You may not agree, but…"

- "I'm just suggesting…"

- "This could be a stupid question, but…"

ACI calls these types of phrases *subservient language* because they say to other people, "I'm not confident with what I'm about to say." The introductory clause announces your lack of forthcoming certainty.

Vocal upticks are equally dismissive habits. This happens when someone raises their vocal tone at the end of a sentence, as if asking a question. The vocal change may also be accompanied by a facial movement, requesting confirmation or approval from the person to whom they're speaking. With this habit, the speaker is again conveying a lack of confidence in what they just said. By simply ending a sentence on a down tone, a speaker conveys their confidence.

Waste Words

Waste words are verbal fillers. Every language has waste words. These are words or phrases someone uses between expressed thoughts. American English examples include um, ah, err, like, you know, hmm, etc.

While many people think the words serve to buy time between meaningful sentences, waste words signify that someone isn't confident (yet) with what they are about to say. That is, they don't know what they want to say next, so they insert a waste word to buy time until their thoughts are organized and ready to be spoken. Some people also believe that waste words allow one person to keep hold of the conversation until they are ready to give up the floor to other people involved. Whether waste words are selfish or substitutes for meaningful conversation, they are distracting—and worse, they convey that the speaker is not confident.

Exorcise Subservient Language and Waste Words

An effective and fun way to rid yourself of these non-confident communication habits is to try the following *exercise*:

1. Find a partner to do this with. It takes less than 2 minutes and you must at least be able to see and hear one another.

2. One person goes first as the storyteller. He/she describes their favorite holiday and why it's their favorite to the listening partner.

3. Anytime the storyteller uses a subservient phrase or waste word, the listener raises his/her hand.

4. Every time the listener raises his/her hand, the storyteller must stop talking and do three (3) very deep knee bends. *(If you physically can't or shouldn't do deep knee bends, contact me for a less physical, but equally tortuous method.)*

5. Once the knee bends are done, the storyteller continues speaking about their favorite holiday.

6. The listener raises his/her hand again if more subservient language or waste words are heard.

7. After 60 seconds, switch roles.

This works so well because it puts your Amygdala on high alert. It focuses on not saying wrong words because it fears the pain and embarrassment of doing deep knee bends! Your Prefrontal Cortex must focus on your speech more than normal, so you will find that you are deliberately speaking slower. After this experience, you'll notice your use of waste words and subservient language diminishes immediately.

You can redo the exercise anytime to get even better results and refresh your verbal control. You will likely start to realize whenever you accidentally use any of this non-confident vocabulary. *Warning*: you will likely be newly frustrated listening to other people who use it. Just refrain from insisting they do deep knee bends!

Breaking Bad with a Buddy

A good way to break any of these bad communication habits is to find a friend or colleague who is willing to help monitor your behavior. When we get anxious, our habits get hard for us to see, let alone control and change. Therefore, it can help to have someone watch and signal you. Arrange a subtle sign like a finger tap on the table or ear lobe for your buddy to make whenever you do the bad habit. Have them monitor you in several situations until you have really unhinged the habit.

Corresponding Confidence

There are entire books written on how to write powerfully using compelling copy and distinctive styles. I offer here just a few rules that specifically help convey confidence in written form:

1.   **Don't be so *sorry*.** Even if your response is delayed, you probably do not need to apologize for being late unless it is past a said deadline or expected timeframe. Studies show that women tend to apologize unnecessarily more than men.[59] Regardless of your gender identity, age, or where you are from, most of us use *sorry* to be polite, well-mannered, and accepted. You may have been brought up culturally to use *sorry* as a means of showing respect.

Start counting the number of *sorries* used in your emails, voicemails, and other interactions to become more aware of how often you use the word. If you remember the previous list of confidence characteristics, taking ownership for your errors and apologizing genuinely is a virtue. Whether we like it or not, someone who overuses the word *sorry* can be construed as weak and not confident.

2.   **Remove subjective qualifiers.** Like subservient language, we often sneak in insecure phrases like "I think," "I believe," "I feel," "it seems," "it's likely," etc. Use these phrases wisely for accuracy but be careful not to diminish your authority. I realize this is not so clear

cut. I also admit it's even been tricky for me to manage it while writing this book! My first book editor was adamant that if you are writing something about which you are an expert or have a strong opinion, you shouldn't water down your statement with disclaimers.

3. **Symbols can mean you're silly.** Exclamation points and emojis are fine to use abundantly with friends and family. Using too many with more formal relationships will make you seem juvenile, especially in business communication. While I never want to stifle anyone's authenticity or enthusiasm, exclamation marks and smiley faces are cute, but don't convey confidence.

4. **Shorter is always better.** For many reasons, it's critical to communicate efficiently. The biggest reason is that people don't have time or interest to read a lot (yes, I realize you are reading a book). Concise, well-written (or well-spoken) communication conveys more confidence because the brevity implies certainty about the content. Unless necessary for accuracy, longer communications lose potency, thereby reducing the reader/listener's attention and perception of the communicator's confidence. Think about any long article, speech, or other communication that started powerfully but lost its verve. You may not even try to read or watch something that is too long. More and more, quick is a key to communicating confidence. It is indeed an art form to condense communication without compromising accuracy or impact.

5. **Grammar matters.** Sloppy writing implies someone doesn't care or is not well-educated. Again, whether we like it or not, erroneous writing may cause other people to lose confidence in you.

As the queen of typos myself, I habitually use multiple spellcheckers, tone and grammar checking tools, even human editors. While that still doesn't catch everything, we should all try our best to make communications accurate and clear.

6. **Avoid making it all about you.** Even if you are writing a cover letter or application about yourself, try not to start multiple

sentences with "I". Also be aware of using too much "me," "my," and "mine." Consider the person reading or listening. Remember that *everyone* wants to feel that they matter. You can stand out just by changing the sentences to seem less about you and more about them. Try to engage the other person by asking for *their* opinion or to share their own experience. Find a way to involve them in the conversation, even if it is one-way in writing.

Unsurprisingly, great interviews are often the ones where the interviewer speaks more than the candidate. Why? Because the interviewer feels that they mattered to the candidate which makes the interviewer feel more confident in themselves. As I hope you now know, giving confidence is a superpower that can be done through all forms of communication.

7. **Don't inflict pain.** In any form of communication, strive to increase other people's confidence by reducing their fear of failure, regret, and rejection— and definitely don't ignite it. As we talked about Confidence Villains previously, creating or elevating fear is a long-common practice in sales, marketing, and negotiation. For example, many sales schools teach how to deliberately uncover or create *buyer pain* (e.g., a major computer company used to proudly teach its salespeople to throw FUD—fear, uncertainty, and doubt— at prospects).

While fear is a powerful motivator, and you may truly have the medicine to help them cure that pain, I challenge you to try to give confidence without having to hurt it first. It is always easier to sell to someone who already confidently knows that they value, need, and want what you offer.

Net Neutral Means Not Personal

When you receive other people's written communications, realize they may not be as aware of the rules above or of their impacts. Most communication is *net neutral*—that is, it is not intended to offend or harm someone else. The communicator is usually oblivious to the effect of their interpreted message. They also don't notice your communication nuances as much as or more than you think. This is what makes miscommunication all too common. We often read too much, or too little, into what people are trying to tell us. When in doubt, ask for clarity and don't let your confidence be unnecessarily kicked.

Conscientious Confident Communication—A Mouthful if You Can Say It Well!

When we consciously convey confidence, it makes a big difference on how other people view, listen to, and remember us. It helps other people trust us faster and more sincerely. Confidence makes us magnetic, attractive, and interesting. It gives us the influence and impact we want. It makes selling and leading so much easier.

Plus, you also know now that confidence is inspiring. By confidently communicating, you will inspire others to stand up, speak up, and be heard, as well. That is a gift you can give every day to people you care about just by communicating with confidence.

Part 5: COACH

Helping Others Be Confident

Coaching someone else formally or informally can be extremely rewarding. You can help them change an undesired habit, achieve a desired goal, or make an important decision. You enable them to become the person they want to be. You empower them with confidence so they can have greater achievement and impact.

What greater purpose can there be?

If you are jumping to this chapter and haven't read (and ideally used) the previous ones, consider this: Would you trust a financial advisor who is poor? Would you seek diet advice from someone who is obese? Would you go to a psychologist if they were always angry? You might be politely curious to listen to what those individuals have to say, but most likely, you will do the opposite of what they suggest. There are certainly great coaches and teachers who can impart valuable knowledge and experience to others. As you probably understand by now, we learn so much about confidence from role models. This doesn't mean that you must be confident all the time. Quite the opposite. It means that you have to be aware of what confidence is and then actively practice what you preach.

Do Unto Yourself First

Whether you realize or like it, you are always being watched by others looking for guidance on how to properly act, react, and interact. You may not be conscious of the observation, but everyone's mirror neurons are always on the lookout for social cues and information (of course some people's more than others). If you are a manager, mentor, teacher, parent, consultant, or coach, you have an even higher level of responsibility. Your title designates you as a *confidence* role model and you are expected to help others become more confident, too.

Any type of guidance is helpful provided the receiver is open to it. Unsolicited advice or proffered observations may trigger a Brain Stem fear causing the person to reject your input, perhaps defensively or aggressively. Their survival response may be the opposite—criticizing themselves deeply, even dangerously. Instead of helping their confidence, your unwanted assistance may harm it.

Therefore, especially if you don't have a formal coaching relationship, be gentle in suggesting that someone increase his/her confidence. Talk about your own experience learning more about confidence and using the tools. Gain their trust by being vulnerable and sharing the benefits you received, and why you needed it. Confide in them so they feel comfortable confiding in you.

Only once you confirm their interest can you then suggest they might also find it valuable. They may not agree at first, again because admitting you want more confidence takes confidence. He/she may ask later, after they've had time for their Prefrontal Cortex to analyze and confidently decide it is a good idea. Be prepared to recommend a specific step such as reading a particular book (this one or another) or article. Suggest they take an assessment you found helpful (Confidence Quotient or another). Always offer to discuss it after they have completed the step(s) and ideally, ask when they would like to do so. Then put a reminder in your calendar to follow up with them. If they are a direct report, you might schedule a follow up meeting.

Congratulations! By following the above simple steps, you are already giving some helpful coaching. Beyond just being helpful, you may be asked or expected to work with someone in a more formal coaching role. Don't panic! You don't have to be certified to do it.

While there are several certification programs, including the one we offer at ACI, coaching programs vary greatly in methodology, time required, and level of scientific/data support. Essentially, there is no one coaching standard or qualification that makes someone a better coach than others. Therefore, anyone can be a coach but not everyone can be a good coach. The best measure by which to judge a coach is whether they can demonstrate relevant, specific, and repeated transformational successes.

Coaching as a Concept

To start being an effective role model and coach, consciously exhibit the visible and behavioral confident characteristics discussed earlier in this book. For example, stand up straight, speak mindfully, and pay attention to other people's verbal and non-verbal communication. Always be growth-minded and insatiably self-aware of your own values, needs, and wants.

Coaches must straddle the fine lines between listener, adviser, friend, and Samaritan. They must have patience, compassion, and open-mindedness. They should never judge, impose their own values, or overlay their own life experiences. What *you* value, what *you* find fun, and what *you* were taught may not be right for *other people*—in fact, it may be the opposite.

Good Coach. Bad Coach.

We've all likely had some form of coaching in our lives, perhaps on a sports team, at the gym, or in a music group. Teachers are coaches, as are parents, friends, relatives, and mostly everyone trying to help you—whether you want it or not.

Regardless of your experience being or working with a coach, you can probably identify some sample characteristics that make someone a good or bad coach.

Good Coaches:

- Work on their own confidence before helping others.

- Listen actively.

- Act as *thought partners*, not as psychoanalysts.

- Stay within a confidence conversation and scope.

- Focus on a goal and help identify options and a game plan to achieve that specific goal.

- Don't offer unsolicited advice or uninformed suggestions.

- Don't assume that any experience of their own or another coachee's is the best solution for the current coachee and situation.

- Don't try to impose their own values or biases.

- Consciously avoid triggering fear of failure, regret, or rejection in coachee.

- Add your additional thoughts here:

____

Bad Coaches:

- Don't model in their own behavior what they are advising others to do.

- Assume they know or can figure out the root cause of someone's personality.

- Try to fix every issue the coachee might have.

- Hunt for problems that the coachee doesn't even realize he/she has.

- Place blame on the coachee for having the issue and reinforce it is the coachee's own fault.

- Criticize without offering help and suggesting viable solutions.

- Intentionally make a coachee feel small, insignificant, and incompetent.

- Convey anger, frustration, disappointment, jealousy, etc. about or to the coachee.

- Ignore, chide, or act indifferently to a coachee's values, needs, and wants.

- Add your additional thoughts here:

____

Reframe your confidence coaching definition away from teaching or leading someone, to acting as their *thought partner.*

Remove any responsibility to shape, direct, lead, or decide someone else's decisions. A coach helps someone figure things out on their own; don't hand them a fish, help them learn to fish. You aren't there to tell someone what to throw out from their closet of thoughts and behaviors, but rather to help them organize it, so they can better see what they have. After they are more aware, they can decide what to keep or change, scaffolded more by your support than your opinion. Most of the time, we already know the answers. We just need some help to access them in our heads and then confirm they are right. Even great coaches use coaches. We all get comfortable living in our own heads amongst the clutter we accumulate as our life stories. Unfortunately, this makes it hard sometimes to clearly see our true values, needs, and wants.

Most of us have been socially taught to *play nicely in the sandbox.* We are taught what is right and wrong, how to be polite, and how to blend in with others.

Regardless of your own orientation and opinion, interacting effectively with other people is undoubtedly complex and can be confidence challenging. Miscommunication causes most interpersonal problems and may even end up as some form of confrontation.

Though a small percentage of people enjoy an awkward confrontation, it isn't fun for most of us. It is even less enjoyable when you are asking someone to confront his/her own bad behaviors. As a coach, this is a tough part of the job. It's much easier if the ask comes from the coachee; it can be very stressful when someone else such as a manager, HR, or parent hires you to help a coachee. Rule #1 in confidence and frankly any other form of coaching is: *to have a way requires the will.*

Your role as a coach isn't to feed compliments or sugar-coat the truth. You can use assessments, tools, or processes to let 3rd parties confirm and communicate your coachee's shortcomings. Be prepared for the coachee to ask if you agree with the generated negative feedback—and assuming you do agree with the findings— be confident in telling the coachee so.

A coach's job is to help someone identify the challenge that is causing them pain or some other unwanted impact. You want to help them understand the impact of ignoring that issue, what they can gain from fixing the problem, and then help them develop a viable plan to conquer that challenge. Ideally, you then help them stay on track to execute the plan, monitor progress, and celebrate successes. It is easier when there is a specific issue or goal, such as losing weight or managing anger.

Coaching can quickly go down unmanageable paths when you are fishing for random challenges and effects. Unless you are a psychoanalyst or have clinical training, be extremely careful to avoid mental-health related issues including depression, extreme mood swings, or an inability to focus. Excuse yourself from the coaching role if someone wants your advice on things outside the goal and/or they want you to diagnose a root cause such as a trauma, childhood experience, or medical condition. Your job is to identify which fear—failure, regret, or rejection—is impacting their confidence and ability to perform optimally. Then you can pinpoint what causes that fear in a specific situation and focus your coaching on helping them overcome that, and only that.

In ACI's Confidence Coaching Certification program, we always emphasize the importance of identifying a specific reason that someone needs confidence coaching, such as nervousness in meetings, presenting to large groups, or networking at a conference. Zero-in on that objective and determine honestly why it is desired. Having a specific issue makes it much easier for you to focus on the best fix and to monitor progress. This enables you both to celebrate critical habit-changing small wins. Once that issue is under control and the goal has been met, you can move on to another.

Confidence Coaching Roadmap

ACI's coaching methodology leans on our Metaconfident Conditioning process noted at the end of the Villains & Kryptonite chapter. In a formal, long-term coaching relationship, you can use all the same tools you used in this book with your coachee. We do encourage you to become an ACI Certified Confidence Coach to ensure you have enough practice and confidence yourself. We teach you how to specifically coach for confidence using this Coaching Roadmap:

1. **Decide** – confirm that the coachee wants to be more confident

2. **Detect** – what the coachee's real problem is (often not the problem presented but more the personal concern)

3. **Decipher** – what is causing the fear and triggering the Amygdala

4. **Determine** – solutions by brainstorming together

5. **Deliberate** – which solution is best through debate, and let the coachee select

6. **Delegate** – offer to help get done and keep the coachee accountable

ACI Confidence Coaching Playbook

In our classes, we use a Confidence Coaching Playbook—a set of conversation questions or prompts—to quickly identify the coachee's confidence issue, the source of his/her fear, and then to help him/her mindfully select the best apparent solution. The final step in the Playbook is for the coach to establish mutually agreed upon accountability check-ins and other support that will help the coachee achieve his/her confidence objective.

The ACI Playbook below provides you with a template for asking safe, productive questions. You may need to take some detours along the way if the coachee isn't forthcoming enough or you uncover some unexpected, important data. The questions should provide you a straight path to gather enough information to start uncovering the confidence challenge and the fear causing it. They will also help you be a good thought partner to figure out options and the desired process to keep your coachee accountable and motivated.

Keep in mind before using these, that you must have the other person's explicit permission to go down this road with them. If they suspect you are coaching them at any time without that agreement, it can cause resentment, anger, future avoidance, and other counterproductive behavior. It can also damage your relationship, making it impossible to help that person at all.

1. Ask an open-ended question to understand the problem from the other person's perspective, *e.g., "How are you feeling about the upcoming presentation?"*

2. Probe for more information about perceived impact and cause, *e.g., "Why are you worried? What do you think might happen?"* Remember that their own perception is their reality, so don't belittle or negate their feelings.

3. Rephrase the problem and impact to get clarity and coachee buy-in, *e.g., "You don't feel you are prepared for the types of questions people might ask you and will lose your credibility. Is that correct?"*

4. Identify which fear(s) is/are being triggered: failure, regret, and/or rejection. Share your findings with the person, *e.g., "It seems that you are worried that you will fail to have all of the answers and be rejected as the expert. Is that accurate?"*

5. Offer to help identify viable solutions, *e.g. "Would it be okay if we brainstormed some potential ways to reduce that fear?"*

6. Assuming they say yes, do some unbiased/creative brainstorming. If they say no, ask if they will come back to you with some ideas of their own, and ask when.

7. Once you have some options, help the coachee pick one they feel is the best. Be sure to reiterate why they feel

this option is the best choice and ask them to confirm that it is, *e.g. "I understand that you feel the best way to reduce your worry is to give the presentation in advance to some of the people for their feedback. Correct?"*

8. Ask how the coachee will know confidently that the goal has been met, *e.g. "How will you know that you have enough of the answers and feel confident to present?"*

9. Ask how you can best support the coachee in reaching their goal, *e.g. "What can I do that would be most helpful to you in achieving this?"*

10. Offer to check-in (in person, by email or text, etc.) with a specific timeline, as well as offer interim support. Ideally schedule the time in both your calendars so it happens, *e.g. "I'd like to meet again in two weeks to check-in and see how things are going. Of course, you can reach out to me before then if you need anything."*

Coaching Matters

Coaching results usually don't happen instantly so give the process a little time to work—just don't be *too* patient. You have an obligation to tell your coachee if the process isn't working. Some people don't respond well to coaching and/or may not be a good fit for your coaching style. A confident coach will recognize that for the well-being of everyone involved.

In all my own experience as a Confidence Coach, I am still often reminded that just by listening to someone, it's possible to make a huge difference in their life. Keeping our mouths shut and judgements turned off helps others feel that they matter. Compassionate listening allows the coachee to organize their own thoughts, recognize how they are feeling, and process thoughts that may otherwise be buried or swirling. In today's chaotic world filled with overchoice, villains, and global pressure, we can ALL use a supportive second brain, an apolitical ally, a confidence coach.

And when you give confidence to others, it shines right back on you. It's renewable and inspires others to be their best, too. It is the gift that gifts you back.

Giving confidence is everyone's superpower and true purpose.

It makes us *all* matter.

Confident Conclusions

When Lynnette and I started ACI back in 2015, we figured we were either completely crazy or fortuitously insightful. We wondered whether there was a way to explain and control confidence from a scientific perspective. Five years later, I can confidently say, "Yes we can."

I have had the blessed opportunity to work with smart, hard-working people from all over the world, from all walks of life. From high performance athletes, to corporate and non-profit professionals, graduate and college students, parents and teens, I've been trusted to help them achieve self-defined success at home and at work.

We have amassed dozens of case studies from audience members, workshop participants, and coaching clients reporting they subsequently obtained dream jobs, promotions, raises, degrees, certificates, and connections. They have started new businesses, found new hobbies, and created high value relationships. They are confidently presenting, networking, contributing, parenting, studying, managing, mentoring, and overall living a life filled with purpose, self-defined value, and pride. They are wealthier, healthier, more engaged, and more productive.

Even more satisfying, they are helping others do the same. They are giving confidence to everyone they care about.

This is what real-life, human superheroes do—and the world so desperately needs more confidence crusaders. Now that you know you can, I hope you'll choose to use your confidence superpowers, too.

A life well lived is one with confidence.

What can you do next?

- Share this book with others you care about. They can order their own print, eBook or audio copy on Amazon. This content is also covered in our eClass, "Be an Everyday Confidence Coach."

- Commit to always improve your Confidence Quotient (CQ).

- Compassionately inspire confidence in others as an informal or ACI Certified Confidence Coach.

- Stay in touch by joining our mailing list and/or social media channels. With open arms, we always welcome new members to the Confidence Community.

- And PLEASE, PLEASE, PLEASE freely share your own experiences and perspectives with us at:

  info@AmericanConfidenceInstitute.com

Thank you for bringing more confidence to the world.

Alyssa

Bibliography

Footnotes

[1] https://simonsinek.com/

[2] American Confidence Institute, Adult Confidence Study, 2015. http://www.americanconfidenceinstitute.com/research-library

[3] Gladwell, Malcolm. *Outliers: The Story of Success*. Little Brown & Co., 2008.

[4] Moura, Rita C., Patricia Maria de Carvalho Aguiar, Graziela Bortz, and Henrique Ballalai Ferraz. "Clinical and Epidemiological Correlates of Task-Specific Dystonia in a Large Cohort of Brazilian Music Players." *Frontiers of Neurology*, 2017 Mar 6, doi: 10.3389/fneur.2017.00073.

[5] https://www.behavioraleconomics.com/resources/mini-encyclopedia-of-be/choice-overload/

[6] Vohs, K. D., Baumeister, R. F., Schmeichel, B. J., Twenge, J. M., Nelson, N. M., & Tice, D. M. (2008). "Making choices impairs subsequent self-control: A limited-resource account of decision making, self-regulation, and active initiative." *Journal of Personality and Social Psychology*, 94, 883-898.

[7] https://www.scientificamerican.com/article/does-social-media-cause-depression/

[8] https://www.simplypsychology.org/maslow.html

[9] http://blog.idonethis.com/the-science-of-motivation-your-brain-on-dopamine/

[10] https://singularityhub.com/2020/01/21/the-brain-predicts-reward-like-an-ai-says-new-deepmind-research/

[11] https://www.health.harvard.edu/mind-and-mood/12-ways-to-keep-your-brain-young

[12] https://www.amazon.com/Teenage-Brain-Neuroscientists-Survival-Adolescents/dp/0062067850

[13] https://www.smithsonianmag.com/science-nature/the-evolution-of-charles-darwin-110234034/

[14] American Confidence Institute Teen Study, 2018. http://www.americanconfidenceinstitute.com/research-library

[15] Dweck, Carol. "What Having a 'Growth Mindset' Actually Means." *Harvard Business Review*, Harvard Business School Publishing Corporation, 2016, thebusinessleadership.academy/wp-content/uploads/2017/03/What-Having-a-Growth-Mindset-Means.pdf.

[16] Walsh, Bryan. "The Upside Of Being An Introvert (And Why Extroverts Are Overrated)." http://www.amysheinbergphd.com, 6 Feb. 2012, www.amysheinbergphd.com/The_Upside_Of_Being_An_Introvert.pdf.

[17] Zani, Mike. "The Predictive Index People Management Study: How to Be a Great Manager (or a Terrible Boss)." *Predictive Index*, June 2018, http://www.predictiveindex.com/wp-content/uploads/2018/08/PI_People-Management-Survey-2018.pdf.

[18] "Dove Self-Esteem Project." *Dove US*, 11 Jan. 2016, http://www.dove.com/us/en/dove-self-esteem-project.html.

[19] L'Oréal Group. "Rebuilding Self-Confidence and Restoring Social Ties - L'Oréal Group: World Leader in Beauty: Official Website." http://www.loreal.com/sustainability/the-l%E2%80%99or%C3%A9al-corporate-foundation/beauty/reaching-out-through-beauty/rebuilding-self-confidence-and-restoring-social-ties.

[20] Mohr, Tara Sophia. "Why Women Don't Apply for Jobs Unless They're 100% Qualified." *Harvard Business Review*, 2 Mar. 2018,

https://hbr.org/2014/08/why-women-dont-apply-for-jobs-unless-theyre-100-qualified.

[21] https://www.myersbriggs.org/my-mbti-personality-type/mbti-basics/home.htm?bhcp=1

[22] https://www.discprofile.com/

[23] https://www.predictiveindex.com/

[24] https://www.thinkxgo.com/

[25] https://wikidiff.com/automatic/autonomic

[26] https://www.memory-key.com/memory/emotion

[27] https://www.psychologytoday.com/us/blog/ulterior-motives/201506/the-consistency-flashbulb-memories

[28] https://www.sciencedirect.com/science/article/pii/S1364661316300997

[29] https://www.robertsapolskyrocks.com/aggression-ii.html

[30] https://www.npr.org/templates/story/story.php?storyId=141164708

[31] https://www.scientificamerican.com/article/is-the-teen-brain-too-rational/

[32] https://www.simplypsychology.org/maslow.html

[33] https://www.psychologytoday.com/us/blog/real-women/201809/the-reality-imposter-syndrome

[34] Mohr, Tara Sophia. "Why Women Don't Apply for Jobs Unless They're 100% Qualified." *Harvard Business Review*, 2 Mar. 2018, https://hbr.org/2014/08/why-women-dont-apply-for-jobs-unless-theyre-100-qualified.

35 https://penntoday.upenn.edu/news/social-media-use-increases-depression-and-loneliness

36 https://thriveglobal.com/stories/benefits-sleep-interview-arianna-huffington/

37 https://www.telegraph.co.uk/films/2019/07/24/inside-keanu-reevess-bullet-time-scene-matrix-changed-cinema/

38 https://newsroom.ucla.edu/releases/Putting-Feelings-Into-Words-Produces-8047

39 https://www.ncbi.nlm.nih.gov/pmc/articles/PMC3651584/

40 Harvard Health Publishing. "The Power of the Placebo Effect." *Harvard Health*, May 2017, www.health.harvard.edu/mental-health/the-power-of-the-placebo-effect.

41 https://www.ncbi.nlm.nih.gov/pmc/articles/PMC3828033/

42 Dweck, Carol. "What Having a 'Growth Mindset' Actually Means." *Harvard Business Review*, Harvard Business School Publishing Corporation, 2016, thebusinessleadership.academy/wp-content/uploads/2017/03/What-Having-a-Growth-Mindset-Means.pdf.

43 https://www.medicalnewstoday.com/articles/326649#epinephrine

44 https://www.self.com/story/how-to-make-your-anxiety-work-for-you-instead-of-against-you

45 http://blog.sirolatrainingmethod.com/2015/08/athletic-stance-4-important-rules-to-have-optimal-position/

46 https://www.forbes.com/sites/kimelsesser/2018/04/03/ power-posing-is-back-amy-cuddy-successfully-refutes-criticism/#690e75b3b8ef

47 https://www.simplypsychology.org/maslow.html

[48] https://theness.com/neurologicablog/index.php/humans-do-not-have-multi-core-processing/

[49] https://www.huffpost.com/entry/youve-been-taking-breaks-n_4453448

[50] https://genius.com/Original-broadway-cast-of-hamilton-aaron-burr-sir-lyrics

[51] https://www.nbcnews.com/better/health/smiling-can-trick-your-brain-happiness-boost-your-health-ncna822591

[52] https://www.webmd.com/balance/stress-management/stress-symptoms-effects_of-stress-on-the-body#1

[53] http://news.mit.edu/2017/stress-can-lead-risky-decisions-1116

[54] Mehrabian, Albert, and Susan R. Ferris. "Inference of Attitudes from Nonverbal Communication in Two Channels." *Journal of Consulting Psychology*, vol. 31, no. 3, 1967, pp. 248–252., doi:10.1037/h0024648.

[55] https://www.businessinsider.com/body-language-indicator-of-confidence-2016-4

[56] https://genius.com/Shakira-hips-dont-lie-lyrics

[57] https://www.sciencedaily.com/releases/2009/10/091005111627.htm

[58] https://flowpsychology.com/defensive-body-language/

[59] https://www.livescience.com/8698-study-reveals-women-apologize.html

Additional Sources of information

Ahammer, Alexander, et al. "Does Confidence Enhance Performance? Causal Evidence from the Field." *Managerial and Decision Economics*, vol. 40, no. 6, 2019, pp. 704–717., doi:10.1002/mde.3038.

Angeletos, George-Marios, et al. "Quantifying Confidence." *SSRN Electronic Journal*, 2014, doi:10.2139/ssrn.2541939.

Belmont, Judith. *Embrace Your Greatness: Fifty Ways to Build Unshakable Self-Esteem*. New Harbinger Publications, 2019.

Birbaumer, Niels, and Jörg Zittlau. *Your Brain Knows More Than You Think: The New Frontiers of Neuroplasticity*. Scribe Publications, 2017.

Bjelland, Julie. *Brain Training for the Highly Sensitive Person: Techniques to Reduce Anxiety and Overwhelming Emotions: an 8-Week Program*. Julie Bjelland, 2017.

Bleidorn, Wiebke, et al. "Age and Gender Differences in Self-Esteem—A Cross-Cultural Window." *Journal of Personality and Social Psychology*, vol. 111, no. 3, 2016, pp. 396–410., doi:10.1037/pspp0000078.

Boldt, Annika, et al. "The Impact of Evidence Reliability on Sensitivity and Bias in Decision Confidence." *Journal of Experimental Psychology: Human Perception and Performance*, vol. 43, no. 8, 2017, pp. 1520–1531., doi:10.1037/xhp0000404.

Brown, Brené. *Dare to Lead: Brave Work, Tough Conversations, Whole Hearts*. Random House Large Print Publishing, 2019.

Carnegie, Dale. *How to Develop Self-Confidence & Influence People by Public Speaking*. Gallery Books, an Imprint of Simon & Schuster, Inc., 2017.

Chan, Yong Kang, and Jessica Bryan. *Empty Your Cup: Why We Have Low Self-Esteem and How Mindfulness Can Help*. Yong Kang Chan, 2017.

Chapman, Mare. *Unshakeable Confidence: The Freedom to Be Our Authentic Selves: Mindfulness for Women*. Mare Chapman, 2017.

Charness, Gary, et al. "Self-Confidence and Strategic Behavior." *Experimental Economics*, vol. 21, no. 1, 2018, pp. 72–98., doi:10.1007/s10683-017-9526-3.

Connolly, Graeme J. "Applying Social Cognitive Theory in Coaching Athletes: The Power of Positive Role Models." *Strategies*, vol. 30, no. 3, 2017, pp. 23–29., doi:10.1080/08924562.2017.1297750.

Davenport, Barrie. *Confidence Hacks: 99 Small Actions to Massively Boost Your Confidence*. Bold Living Press, 2014.

Dryden, Windy. *Cognitive-Emotive-Behavioural Coaching: A Flexible and Pluralistic Approach*. Routledge, 2017.

Gazipura, Aziz. *Not Nice: Stop People Pleasing, Staying Silent, & Feeling Guilty … and Start Speaking Up, Saying No, Asking Boldly, and Unapologetically Being Yourself*. B.C. Allen Publishing & Tonic Books, 2017.

Gazipura, Aziz. *The Art of Extraordinary Confidence: Your Ultimate Path to Love, Wealth, and Freedom*. B.C. Allen Publishing, 2016.

Greenberg, Melanie. *The Stress-Proof Brain: Master Your Emotional Response to Stress Using Mindfulness and Neuroplasticity*. New Harbinger Publications, 2017.

Haden, Jeff. *The Motivation Myth: How High Achievers Really Set Themselves up to Win*. Portfolio/Penguin, 2018.

Hanson, Rick. *Resilient: How to Grow an Unshakable Core of Calm, Strength, and Happiness*. Harmony Crown, 2018.

Hawi, Nazir S., and Maya Samaha. "The Relations Among Social Media Addiction, Self-Esteem, and Life Satisfaction in University Students." *Social Science Computer Review*, vol. 35, no. 5, 2016, pp. 576–586., doi:10.1177/0894439316660340.

Hazeldine, Simon. *Neuro-Sell: How Neuroscience Can Power Your Sales Success*. Kogan Page, 2014.

Helmstetter, Shad. *Negative Self-Talk and How to Change It*. Park Avenue Press, 2019.

Ho, Judy. *Stop Self-Sabotage: Six Steps to Unlock Your True Motivation, Harness Your Willpower, and Get Out of Your Own Way*. HarperWave, an Imprint of HarperCollins Publishers, 2019.

Hsieh, Wei-Fen, et al. "Confidence Identification Based on the Combination of Verbal and Non-Verbal Factors in Human Robot Interaction." *2019 International Joint Conference on Neural Networks (IJCNN)*, 2019, doi:10.1109/ijcnn.2019.8851845.

Jaynes, Sharon. *Enough: Silencing the Lies That Steal Your Confidence*. Harvest House Publishers, 2018.

Jewell, Louisa. *Wire Your Brain for Confidence: The Science of Conquering Self-Doubt*. Famous Warrior Press, 2017.

Johnson, Jill J. *Compounding Your Confidence: Strategies to Expand Your Opportunities for Success*. Johnson Consulting Services, 2018.

Kay, Katty, and Claire Shipman. *The Confidence Code: The Science and Art of Self-Assurance—What Women Should Know*. Harper Business, an Imprint of HarperCollins Publishers, 2018.

Killelea, Grace. *The Confidence Effect: Every Woman's Guide to the Attitude That Attracts Success*. American Management Association, 2016.

Konnikova, Maria. *The Confidence Game: Why We Fall for It . . . Every Time*. Penguin Books, an Imprint of Penguin Random House LLC, 2017.

Ladge, Jamie J., et al. "Retaining Professionally Employed New Mothers: The Importance of Maternal Confidence and Workplace Support to Their Intent to Stay." *Human Resource Management*, vol. 57, no. 4, 2017, pp. 883–900., doi:10.1002/hrm.21889.

Liu, Wenqi, et al. "Group Decision-Making Based on Heterogeneous Preference Relations with Self-Confidence." *Fuzzy Optimization and Decision Making*, vol. 16, no. 4, 2017, pp. 429–447., doi:10.1007/s10700-016-9254-8.

Liu, Xia, et al. "A Group Decision Making Approach Considering Self-Confidence Behaviors and Its Application in Environmental

Pollution Emergency Management." *International Journal of Environmental Research and Public Health*, vol. 16, no. 3, 2019, p. 385., doi:10.3390/ijerph16030385.

Liu, Xia, et al. "Social Network Group Decision Making: Managing Self-Confidence-Based Consensus Model with the Dynamic Importance Degree of Experts and Trust-Based Feedback Mechanism." *Information Sciences*, vol. 505, 2019, pp. 215–232., doi:10.1016/j.ins.2019.07.050.

Manson, Mark. *The Subtle Art of Not Giving a Fuck: A Counterintuitive Approach to Living a Good Life*. HarperOne, 2016.

Markway, Barbara G., and Celia Ampel. *The Self-Confidence Workbook: A Guide to Overcoming Self-Doubt and Improving Self-Esteem*. Althea Press, 2018.

Marshall, James A.R., et al. "Individual Confidence-Weighting and Group Decision-Making." *Trends in Ecology & Evolution*, vol. 32, no. 9, 2017, pp. 636–645., doi:10.1016/j.tree.2017.06.004.

McCarthy, Scott, et al. "Corporate Social Responsibility and CEO Confidence." *Journal of Banking & Finance*, vol. 75, 2017, pp. 280–291., doi:10.1016/j.jbankfin.2016.11.024.

McGrane, Bronagh, et al. "The Relationship between Fundamental Movement Skill Proficiency and Physical Self-Confidence among Adolescents." *Journal of Sports Sciences*, vol. 35, no. 17, 2016, pp. 1709–1714., doi:10.1080/02640414.2016.1235280.

McKay, Matthew, and Patrick Fanning. *Self-Esteem: A Proven Program of Cognitive Techniques for Assessing, Improving, and Maintaining Your Self-Esteem*. New Harbinger Publications, 2016.

McKay, Sarah, and Travis Kemp. "Neuroscience and Coaching." *Positive Psychology Coaching in Practice*, 2018, pp. 57–67., doi:10.4324/9781315716169-4.

Minzlaff, Kathrine A. "Organisational Coaching: Integrating Motivational Interviewing and Mindfulness with Cognitive Behavioural Coaching." *Coaching: An International Journal of*

Theory, Research, and Practice, vol. 12, no. 1, 2018, pp. 15–28., doi:10.1080/17521882.2018.1478437.

Monahan, Heather. *Confidence Creator*. Boss in Heels, 2018.

Morris, Deborah Gray. *Calculate with Confidence*. Elsevier, 2018.

Neff, Kristin, and Christopher K. Germer. *The Mindful Self-Compassion Workbook: A Proven Way to Accept Yourself, Build Inner Strength, and Thrive*. Guilford Press, 2018.

Neff, Kristin. *Self-Compassion: The Proven Power of Being Kind to Yourself*. William Morrow, an Imprint of HarperCollins Publishers, 2015.

Passmore, Jonathan. *Mastery in Coaching: A Complete Psychological Toolkit for Advanced Coaching*. Kogan Page, 2014.

Phillips, Cristy. "Lifestyle Modulators of Neuroplasticity: How Physical Activity, Mental Engagement, and Diet Promote Cognitive Health during Aging." *Neural Plasticity*, vol. 2017, 2017, pp. 1–22., doi:10.1155/2017/3589271.

Pooler, Jennifer A., et al. "Cooking Matters for Adults Improves Food Resource Management Skills and Self-Confidence Among Low-Income Participants." *Journal of Nutrition Education and Behavior*, vol. 49, no. 7, 2017, doi:10.1016/j.jneb.2017.04.008.

Rahayu, Titik, and Kamisah Osman. "Knowledge Level and Self-Confidence on The Computational Thinking Skills Among Science Teacher Candidates." *Jurnal Ilmiah Pendidikan Fisika Al-Biruni*, vol. 8, no. 1, 2019, pp. 117–126., doi:10.24042/jipfalbiruni.v8i1.4450.

Ratiu, Lucia, et al. "Developing Managerial Skills Through Coaching: Efficacy of a Cognitive-Behavioral Coaching Program." *Journal of Rational-Emotive & Cognitive-Behavior Therapy*, vol. 34, no. 4, 2016, pp. 244–266., doi:10.1007/s10942-016-0256-9.

Ryan, Richard M., and Edward L. Deci. *Self-Determination Theory: Basic Psychological Needs in Motivation, Development, and Wellness*. The Guilford Press, 2018.

Sandefer, Laura A. *Courage to Grow: How Acton Academy Turns Learning Upside Down*. Greenleaf Book Group LLC, 2018.

Shaffer, Joyce. "Neuroplasticity and Clinical Practice: Building Brain Power for Health." *Frontiers in Psychology*, vol. 7, 2016, doi:10.3389/fpsyg.2016.01118.

Silberstein, Laura R. *How to Be Nice to Yourself: The Everyday Guide to Self-Compassion: Effective Strategies to Increase Self-Love and Acceptance*. Althea Press, 2019.

Smith, Fraser. *The Complete Brain Exercise Book: Train Your Brain: Improve Memory, Language, Motor Skills & More + A Health & Diet Plan with 125 Recipes*. Firefly Books Ltd, 2015.

Southwick, Steven M., and Dennis Charney. *Resilience: The Science of Mastering Life's Greatest Challenges*. Cambridge University Press, 2018.

Surya, Edy, et al. "Improving Mathematical Problem-Solving Ability and Self-Confidence of High School Students Through Contextual Learning Model." *Journal on Mathematics Education*, vol. 8, no. 1, 2016, doi:10.22342/jme.8.1.3324.85-94.

Uzman, Ersin, and Ilknur Maya. "Self-Leadership Strategies as the Predictor of Self-Esteem and Life Satisfaction in University Students." *International Journal of Progressive Education*, vol. 15, no. 2, 2019, pp. 78–90., doi:10.29329/ijpe.2019.189.6.

Vullioud, Colin, et al. "Confidence as an Expression of Commitment: Why Misplaced Expressions of Confidence Backfire." *Evolution and Human Behavior*, vol. 38, no. 1, 2017, pp. 9–17., doi:10.1016/j.evolhumbehav.2016.06.002.

Whalen, Sean. *How to Make Sh*t Happen: Make More Money, Get in Better Shape, Create Epic Relationships, and Control Your Life!* CreateSpace Publishing, 2018.

White, Krista A., et al. "Extern Programs Promote Confidence and Reduce Anxiety With Clinical Decision Making in Nursing Students." *Nurse Educator*, vol. 44, no. 5, 2019, pp. 239–244., doi:10.1097/nne.0000000000000625.

Wien, Anders Hauge, and Svein Ottar Olsen. "Producing Word of Mouth – a Matter of Self-Confidence? Investigating a Dual Effect of Consumer Self-Confidence on WOM." *Australasian Marketing Journal (AMJ)*, vol. 25, no. 1, 2017, pp. 38–45., doi:10.1016/j.ausmj.2017.01.005.

Acknowledgements

Writing a book challenges confidence in unimaginable ways. When people compare it to having a baby, I can't agree because I've done both multiple times. With a new baby, you don't have control of *what* is born (at least not with current available technology). When your baby is born, you're excited to mold that infant into a self-functioning person who you hope will reflect your values and legacy. Unlike babies, with a book you decide everything before it's even born: every word, every reference, every punctuation mark, every picture, your bio, the title, the testimonials, the format and more. When the book is born, it doesn't just resemble you, it is a version of you.

Books and babies do have something very much in common: they invite abundant unsolicited criticism. Anyone who has a child or has been a child, read a book or thought about writing one, is a self-appointed expert. And despite knowing they usually have well-intended feedback, it is still very tough to hear that someone thinks your creation isn't perfect. Worse, with a book the criticism is often public, unfixable, and permanently damaging to your business. Obviously with seven published so far, I still find the accomplishment worthwhile. If you aspire to be an author, get your confidence armor on. You're going to need it.

Therefore, my final bit of confidence advice (whether you are writing a book or not) is to create a virtual posse. They don't need to be your friends or even people you've ever met in person. Just identify people who like who you are and want to be in your orbit. Unofficially, make them your personal Board of Advisors. Proactively reach out to them when you need renewed faith in your work and yourself. Lean on them to refuel you. Allow them to give you confidence and be sure to thank them for it. Maybe one of the best aspects of writing a book is that you get to thank your posse using indelible print – just as I am about to do here…

Choice was significantly more demanding than my previous six books. I had more knowledge, time, and conviction that this book needed to be *the one*. I let it stew for three years, wrote it, trashed it, then wrote it again. I beta, gamma, delta, and zeta tested all the tools and messages. I tested my own patience as well as my family's and friends' while I wallowed through valleys of frustration and eons of isolation.

I start with sincere thanks to my older son, Zak. Without him, I would never have gotten into brain science. His neurological condition ignited my maternal motivation, but it has been his continuous willingness to be part of this journey which has continued to fuel my mission. His help editing this book cannot be thanked by mere words. Zak's insights and corrections have made me a better writer, a more accurate teacher, and an incredibly proud mom.

My younger son, Ben, was gifted with extraordinary emotional intelligence that fuels my faith and hope for all mankind. He drives me to be a better person in all ways. I argue in this book that confidence is learned; however, I do believe that some things are clearly divine. Ben came to this iteration of life with an abundance of wisdom and grace that unobtrusively teaches everyone around him how to be authentically compassionate and purposely positive.

Jeff, my husband, is unbelievably supportive. I totally appreciate that he manages our household to free me to selfishly follow my passions. More than that, he is the source of my confidence every day, especially when entrepreneurial troughs or thoughtless people mash down my mojo.

I am also honored to have the company of ACI's Certified Confidence Coaches and other loyal Confidence Crusaders. I keep all your feedback forms, social posts, and emails in my confidence collection. The continued interest and active support keep ME confident, knowing that I am doing something that matters.

To my incredibly talented niece Ally Tuttelman, who made the confidence-creating cover. You are beautiful in all ways, including your ability to bring more beauty to the world through thoughtful art and design. I'm also very proud of my nephew Josh to whom I gladly hand off the family *brainiac* title as he forges ahead to be the incredible engineer and musician that I didn't have the confidence to be.

To Andrew Siff who helped me to be confidently accurate and well-referenced. Lawler Kang for his incredibly generous editorial work, long time allyship, and for always encouraging me to fly despite the absence of a visible net.

To my own confidants: Pam Micznik, Marco Emrich, Julianne Zimmerman, Roberta Matuson, Pam Bakos, Kathryn Rose, Bobbie Carlton, Kim Levings, Lori Siragusa, Stephanie Marks, Toni Spitzer, Jane Greenstein, my mom Nancy Dver and my unofficial godmother, Susan Morin. Sisters can be many things, but mine is incredibly insightful and fantastically fun. I wouldn't be confident enough to try to be her friend so I'm thankful for the genetic privilege to hang out with Jen Tuttelman.

I'm still not sure what I did to deserve such amazing people in my life, let alone when real-life angels show up like Kristin Deegan and Aimee Broadhurst. I do believe that the friendships which started from business transactions quickly glued us together at a subconscious, lifelong soul-sisters level. Your attitudes, vast talents, and inspiring presence have given me more confidence than you'll ever know. I am so grateful beyond what I could ever express or imagine I could ever repay.

And as crazy as I realize this may sound, I am grateful for my quirky rescue dog, Georgie. He keeps me company while I think and write, provides oxytocin-activating snuggles, and Oedipal loyalty that makes me feel like a Confidence Queen. Yeah, you can even get confidence from a canine.

May this book be homage to all the heart-guided, head-smart people (and pets!) who are committed to make this world happier, healthier, and more confident.

"'Finding yourself' is not really how it works. You aren't a ten dollar bill in last winter's coat pocket.

You are also not lost. Your true self is right there, buried under cultural conditioning, other people's opinions, and inaccurate conclusions you drew as a kid that became your beliefs about who you are.

'Finding yourself' is actually returning to yourself.

An unlearning, an excavation, a remembering who you were before the world got its hands on you."

— Emily McDowell

Small Group Book Discussion Guide

To access a downloadable copy of all the templates/tools in the book, go to:
www.AmericanConfidenceInstitute.com/Toolkit

Here are some book discussion exercises and prompts to use as further learning in small groups.

If you're interested in having Alyssa or another ACI member participate in your discussion (onsite or virtual), please contact us. We love to do this and do it frequently.

Some of the exercises in the book that work well to share and discuss in a group:

- **Confident Role Models**: Describe confident and not confident people you know/knew

- **Structure**: Share one you already use or will use in the future whenever you need some instant confidence

- **Three Little Things**: What are yours?

- **Inside Out Pet Peeves**: Pick one of your own, turn it inside out, and find the value transgression in it

- Perform the **Waste Words** removal 'exorcise' with partners

Prompt Questions for Group Discussions

1. Share a confident experience or accomplishment from the past. How did it make you feel then? How does it make you feel now?

2. What do you think are the general differences between most men and women in how they show confidence? Are there differences in how they generally walk, sit, or stand? How about the ways they talk, listen, or communicate overall?

3. How does the way a person dress impact their own confidence? How does it impact other people's confidence?

4. Why do you think "caveperson" behavior (bully, bonehead, imposter) is often rewarded?

5. What do you think are the long-term implications to people who are intimidated/bullied by someone else's "caveperson" behavior? What about the long-term implications to the bully?

6. What is one sign that a lack of confidence is holding you/your organization/your team back? What is the impact both in the short and long-term? What are some potential ways to address it? What is the best way?

7. Which confidence tool, technique, or tip did you like best in this book or anywhere else? Why?

8. Who is one person needing confidence that you can help and how?

American Confidence Institute Information

www.AmericanConfidenceInstitute.com

- **Onsite or Online Keynotes & Workshops**
  - Confidence is a Choice

    Keynotes = 1-1.5 hours; Workshops = 3-4 hours

  - A Pitch is Not a Presentation (1 day)

    includes 1x1 coaching for all participants

  - Everyday Confidence Coaching (1 day)

    includes ACI Confidence Coaching Certification

    Tailored for the specific audience and event. Always interactive, entertaining, engaging, and immediately applicable.

- **Books—Paperback, eBook, Audiobook** | *Available on Amazon.com. Contact us for bulk order discounts.*

- **Confidence Quotient (CQ)** | *Online assessment purchasable as single use or discounted bundled licenses available.*

- **eClass** | *"How to be an Everyday Confidence Coach" Online, on-demand, self-paced. Approximately 3 hours total learning time.*

- **1x1 Coaching** | *Let us match you to one of our Certified Confidence Coaches. Delivered in person or online.*

- **Confidence Coaching Certification** | *No coaching experience necessary. ACI eClass + online exam + 3-hour Practicum. Approximately 6 hours total learning time. All online!*

You can download all the tools within the book here:

www.AmericanConfidenceInstitute.com/Toolkit

<u>Other FREE resources on the ACI website:</u>

- **ACI's Research Library**

- **In Confidence Podcast**

- **Blog**

- **Monthly emails**

- **ACI social media posts**—Follow us on your favorite channel:

  Email: info@AmericanConfidenceInstitute.com
  Twitter: @ConfidenceInst
  LinkedIn: /company/americanconfidenceinstitute
  Facebook: /@ConfidenceInst
  YouTube: American Confidence Institute
  Instagram: /ConfidenceInst

Made in the USA
Middletown, DE
07 November 2020